Medicine on Waves
-The Diary of a Ship's Surgeon-

Self-publication

printed by
Book Printing UK,
Remus House
Coltsfoot Drive
Woodston
Peterborough PE2 9BF

First published 2021

Set in Times New Roman 12 / 14 pt and Bradley Hand ITC 14 pt

A CIP catalogue record for this book is available from the British Library

ISBN: 978-1-5272-8360-2

For my wife Fei,
my Sisters
and all my Friends

The Author

Dr. Werner Schomburg

...grew up in Hanover, Germany, where he also graduated from medical school in 1994. He spent his junior doctor years in England before emigrating to Australia. There he worked on the beautiful island of Tasmania for four years. As a Senior House Officer, he held positions in a variety of specialties including Accident and Emergency and Intensive Care.

He returned to England to complete his training to become a General Practitioner (GP). As a trainee he joined a practice in Cornwall and qualified in 2000. He then worked for his training practice until he gained a position as a Ship's Physician with Carnival Cruise Lines in 2002. This book is about his first journey as a ship's doctor.

After three years of service for Carnival, he settled in London to work as a GP. As he had acquired the taste for travel he started to work all over the world for a medical Air Rescue Company. During his travels for the company he met his wife, Fei Chen, in Beijing. They were married in 2016.

Between his international assignments he found the time to qualify as an Aviation Physician with the Royal Air Force. At the time of writing he is under contract to provide services as a military physician for the Army and Air Force.

One Year On

Being back onboard a ship, everything feels very familiar. As a matter of fact, it seems that nothing has changed since my first assignment as a ship's physician. The daily routine is well known to me. Even the ship I am sailing on, the M/S Holiday, *is very familiar to me. It is of the same class as the* Jubilee *and has consequently the same layout. So, getting around my present vessel feels almost like being on the "good old Jube".*

My diary as a ship's physician, which you are about to read, has been mainly written during my time onboard the M/S Jubilee *from February to August 2002. But towards the end of my contract I became too busy (and too tired) to keep up with events. So, I used part of my shore leave to finish it. That was hard going at times. Writing can be a very tiring and exhausting activity. I found it emotionally demanding to go through some of my experiences again. But I was determined to finish this diary. After many hours of typing on the computer during various mornings, afternoons or evenings and with many cups of tea and coffee, I succeeded.*

So here it is. One year on. And it is as current as today, since not much changed over the last twelve months. I hope you find it stimulating to read.

Werner Schomburg   *Onboard the M/S* Holiday
                                                                            2 February 2003

Author's Note

Rediscovery

Dear Reader,

To publish this diary was always in the back of my mind, but I struggled to find the time to edit my writing to give it the right shape to be printed.

With the arrival of the Coronavirus and the subsequent lockdown I suddenly had some extra time on my hand. There was not much one could do during leisure times. Theatres, museums, restaurants...everything was closed. I even was prevented from playing my beloved game of golf as all courses and driving ranges were shut down.

So, I embarked on my first journey as a ship's doctor again by revising the lines I had written almost 20 years ago. I smelled the fresh sea air again, remembered friends and colleagues, and the challenges which came with my first assignment as a ship's physician on the M/S Jubilee. It turned out to be really fun to (virtually) travel around the Caribbean Sea again.

Nowadays, we live in a very different world. The ease of going anywhere one wants and doing whatever one likes is gone. To plan, book and register ahead appears to be essential for almost every leisure activity these days. And the ability to travel around the world is still very limited due to border controls and restrictions concerning air travel.

So, I invite you to step onboard the M/S Jubilee. Travel with me to the United States and from there around the Caribbean Sea. Share the highlights (and frustrations) of being a Ship's Doctor with me. Times have changed dramatically since the spring of last year. Let's look back at some of "the good old times".

London, June 2021

Dr. Werner Schomburg
DrSchomb@yahoo.co.uk

Flying or not Flying?

The day had come. I had arrived at Düsseldorf Airport, tired but prepared. Many weeks had passed, filled with thinking and doing. Finally, I had said "Good-bye" to friends and family and there I was – ready to go. But the beginning of my travels turned out to be a non-starter. The girl at the Lufthansa desk refused to give me the ticket, because I couldn't produce a seafarer's book. I persuaded her to send an e-mail to the office in the US to clarify the situation. But what use would that be? It was 3 a.m. in the United States at that moment. The girl asked me to come back in an hour. But I was sure that nothing would happen during the next hour. I pondered what to do. Then I remembered: I had the mobile phone number of my boss in the US. But would he be happy to hear from me at 3 a.m. in the morning? But "flying or not flying" – that was the question. So I made the call. A sleepy voice answered and I explained the situation to him. He promised to call the airline office in the US to fix the problem. After that I lingered around the Lufthansa desk waiting for good news.

Good-bye, my friends

And eventually it came. "Here is your ticket. "Have a good flight" said the Lufhansa girl and gave me the flight ticket. Check-in went smoothly and the fact that my suitcase had a weight of 34 kg was not a problem. But I asked myself, will I see it ever again? Then I hopped onto the plane. Twenty minutes later I was in Frankfurt. There, I had to go through another security check. The usual procedure took place: removing the laptop from its case, taking off of my shoes and belt, and walking with slipping-down trousers and in socks through the metal detector. Well, the events of 9/11 certainly took the fun out of flying. On the other hand, drinks on the plane were served from glass bottles. Break one and it makes a knife-like weapon. And the ballpoint pen I had on me was also sharp and pointy. I think all this security stuff is just for appearance, to make us passengers feel better.

Some In-Flight Fun

Finally, I was onboard the plane, jetting towards Washington DC. After drinks and food, I had a chat with my seat neighbour, a young gentleman. He had just returned from a holiday in Italy. Then there was a movie to watch, the usual crime and action stuff. I was just getting cosy when I heard an announcement: "Is there a doctor on board?" Well, I am one, so I raised my arm. The purser came and explained the situation to me. There was a semi-conscious passenger. They found an empty container for tablets on him and the purser was wondering what he had taken. Was it something dangerous? Together we went to the passenger concerned. I tried to talk to the guy but he was not co-operative, just muttered "Go away!"

Well, at least he was somewhat conscious and responsive, but obviously drunk. I checked the empty tablet container. It was for "benzoes" (Benzodiazepine, a kind of sleeping pill). That would keep him quiet for a while, but hopefully not too quiet as it also suppresses breathing. I recruited a fellow passenger as a guard. He was a big and solid man, more than capable of keeping this guy under control. It turned out that the drunk passenger was from the Ukraine, but had become an American citizen. He was on his way back home to the US.

We found also two empty bottles of vodka on him. I suppose that had knocked him out. I released the "guard" from his duties. I frequently reassured myself that my newly acquired patient was still breathing while I had a chat with the purser. She had spent 10-odd years in the flying business. This kind of incident happened more often recently, she told me. The Scandinavians are the worst. They can't handle the booze. Because alcohol is so expensive in their countries, they are not used to it. Then we talked about what lay ahead. She was going to have a day off in Washington DC, then flying back the next day. Afterwards, she would have a few days off duty before the next assignment. That was her lifestyle. Well, I didn't know anything about my future lifestyle (on the ship). All I knew at that stage was that I have to change planes in Washington DC.

In my home town
Hanover, Germany

I was stuck with the Ukrainian patient for the rest of the flight. I made sure that he remained in a satisfactory state. Well, I suppose that was part of being a doctor: always on duty. But I was looking forward to be relieved of my responsibility after landing. Finally, touchdown in Washington DC. All the passengers were leaving, except for the patient and myself. Then paramedics appeared, together with a few solid guys from airport security and two police officers. All this had been arranged in advance by the captain of the plane. Facing the heavy man-power the Ukrainian had no chance to cause trouble. He was sleepy and unhappy but OK. I handed him over to the authorities. Then I was free to leave. The crew members bestowed on me a big bottle of champagne, as well as chocolates and other goodies. That was their way of saying thank you.

Welcome to America
In the immigration area of the airport I was asked to step into a side room. The interior was very plain, just furnished with a few rows of plastic chairs and a desk with a huge US flag behind it. In the corner was a TV showing CNN news. The reports were mainly about crime and violence. Welcome to America. I took a seat. Around me were a few men. A quick chat with my seat neighbour revealed that he was from Croatia. He was a seaman, due to join a ship in New Orleans. The other men were from Malaysia, Russia, India and other countries – all sailors. It seemed this place was for seafarers only. Then I heard a stern call from the

immigration officer at the desk: "Mr. Schomburg, please!" I had to answer few questions about my purpose for coming to the US. The tone of the officer's voice changed immediately, once he inquired about my profession. He remarked: "Oh, you are a doctor. Well, Doctor Schomburg, have a seat. It won't be long".

Five minutes later I left the room with the required paperwork. I claimed my baggage and went through customs. Afterwards I checked-in for my connecting flight to Miami, Florida. After a security check I had a long walk through endless corridors to get to the departure gate. There I was faced with another security inspection. At that point I felt totally stuffed – hot, sweaty, tired and thirsty. I was definitely not in a mood for yet another document and luggage inspection. A young officer walked along the waiting line at the gate, looking for another victim to conduct a random check. I looked straight at him. It seemed to work. He didn't bother me.

Finally, I took my seat onboard the plane, next to an elderly lady. We started the usual conversation between strangers. Where are you from? What are you doing? Oh, you are going to join a ship. How exciting! The lady had been born in Cuba but was a proud American. She had nothing but total admiration for the US. America is best! She was flying home to join the huge population of exiled Cubans in Miami. On my way from the airport to the hotel I met another enthusiast of "god's own country". The taxi driver in Miami didn't stop to tell me that America is great and full of opportunities. Well, that may be true if you don't look too closely around you. Just forget the rundown communities, the homeless people and the violent crime in this country. But one thing is true about America: everything is big. The cars, the hotel rooms, even the Burger I ordered. But my exhaustion was equally big and I fell asleep halfway through my dinner.

Biscayne Bay
Miami, Florida, USA

Thursday, 7th of February 2002
Miami, Florida

First, meet the Lawyer
When I woke up, I asked myself, *where am I?* I stepped out onto the balcony. From there I could see a large bay, bridges and a causeway. There was also a marina nearby with a lot of fancy boats. It was Miami, Florida at 6:30 in the morning. I was on a tight schedule that day. It was short-sleeve weather and I had breakfast on the hotel veranda. I should have known that I had ordered too much food. The omelette was not big, but huge. Over a mug of coffee, I read my contract again. A lot of lawyer's talk. For that reason I had it checked by a lawyer before

departure. A solicitor from the BMA (British Medical Association) had it looked over and had told me that it was reasonable. A lot of clauses were in favour of the company (Carnival Cruise Lines) but the money was OK.

At 10:00 a.m. I was picked up by a company driver. After a short ride through a jungle of highways and freeways we arrived at the company's headquarters (HQ). It was a huge compound with thousands of employees. After signing in at the main desk, I was given a badge which said "Crew". Well, that's what I was at the time. I heard a lot of "Hello, nice to meet you!" and saw a lot of new faces. My first meeting was not with my boss or colleagues, but with a lawyer. There was no talk about ships or medicine. The topic was how to avoid litigation. I received good advice, such as: be thorough, document well, order a test if you are not sure. And much more…I knew that America was the land of litigation. But was it really that bad? Maybe so. I was then introduced to Erika. She was the assistant Medical Director. Steve, the director and my boss, was not present at the time. He was on official business in Salt Lake City, where the Winter Olympics were held at the time. Erika and I discussed all the relevant topics: ships regulations, the onboard pharmacy, medical guidelines and how to evacuate emergencies by helicopter. During the meeting, a man stuck his head into the office. He asked Erika if he could talk to her for a moment. "It's about the upcoming court case", he announced. I wondered: will my new job be fun? Doubts crept in. But Erika reassured me: "You will be fine. Just be careful. But enjoy your job!"

Scary Training

I had my lunch in the canteen before the final bit of the introduction. In the last session I learnt to operate the biohazard device. This machine was able to check for any dangerous powders. It could determine whether something contained Anthrax (a lethal bacterium), or not. There had been some incidences on the cruise ships where white powder was found in public areas. So far, all of them had been hoaxes but it was the responsibility of the medical team to test for such substances. In order to do that, I would need to jump into a spacesuit. That didn't sound like fun. But the world had changed since September 11, 2001. My session with Erika ended around 4 pm. The final part of my initiation took place in the basement. It housed the clothing store where my measurements were taken for an officer's uniform. And that was it. I was driven back to the hotel. I had two free days ahead of me before joining the *M/S Victory* on Sunday, 10 February.

Friday, 8th of February 2002
Miami, Florida

Driving with No Driver

My breakfast came with a copy of the newspaper *USA Today*, which was full of articles about the Enron scandal. A lot of lies and manipulations had taken place and then the company had gone bust. The big guys made money and the small guys lost it. It was one of the usual stories.

What to do with this day? I decided to go for a harbour cruise. I hopped on a boat for a two-hour tour. It also passed the quay for cruise ships. The commentary explained that Miami is the world busiest harbour for cruise ships and a lot of shipping companies operate here but the Carnival is the biggest. Then we entered the residential area of the bay. There the boat passed the homes of the rich and famous: Elizabeth Taylor, Arnold Schwarzenegger, Jack Nicholson. A home on the waterfront with a pool and a private marina could cost easily $30,000,000 – so we were told. Hmm, let's see. A maid at the hotel where I was staying earned about $5 per hour. So, she would have to work roughly 3,000 years to afford such a house.

(Assuming she works 40 hours per week and had no unnecessary expenses such as food or clothing.)

On the Metro Mover, Miami

After the boat ride, I travelled to the centre of Miami by Metromover, an automated train system. No driver was on board, so one has to believe in technology. I got off somewhere downtown. Everything was in Spanish there: the signs, the posters and the language of the people in the streets. Even the teller in the *Bank of America* greeted me in Spanish. But then switched to English when I looked at him in bewilderment. English was certainly not the first language in that part of Miami. But I managed. I got a haircut and bought a pair of shoes. They had to be white to match the uniform I was about to wear. Ordering a sandwich at a deli was a bit tricky though. The shop assistant didn't speak any English so I just pointed at the stuff I wanted to go into my sandwich. Luckily, the cash register spoke mathematics – showing the amount to pay in digits.

Opening Ceremony,
Winter Olympics, 2002

Olympia – The Show begins

Back at the hotel I watched my favourite TV show, *Frasier*. Frasier is a kind of colleague: a neurotic radio psychiatrist who lives in Seattle, played by the actor Kelsey Grammer. At 8 pm I watched the Opening Ceremony of the Winter Olympics. There were held on US soil at the time – in Salt Lake City, Utah. I couldn't decide what was more annoying: the frequent commercials or the patriotism dripping from the screen. Maybe it was a fallout from the events of 9/11. The actual flag from the World Trade Centre was presented during the ceremony.

Yeah, yeah, everybody was proud to be an American. And then the president of the United States, George W. Bush, appeared. The words he spoke only made sense in parts of his speech. But he had good PR (public relations) advisors. I think it was a neat idea to let him sit casually among the US athletes. The signal was clear: I am with them in their fight for the medals.

What followed was the Olympic oath with all this *b-shit* about fairness, etc. In reality, the athletes had just finished their course of doping. And the lucrative advertising contracts were already drafted, ready to be signed by the athletes – but just by the ones who would win. Then followed the endless marching-in of the participants. Afterwards, a string of meaningless interviews was shown. "How did it feel to carry the Olympic flame?" "Just great!"… and so on. I drank a whole bottle of champagne with the show. It was the reward for my helping the drunk guy on the plane. It felt good – until I had to listen to this drivel. At that moment I had enough and went off to bed.

Sunday, 10th of February 2002
Miami, Florida, USA

Ship Ahoy!
It was the big day. I was about to join "my" ship, the *M/S Victory*. The vessel was built with a capacity for 3,030 passengers and had a crew of 1,209 men and women. There she was, sitting at the quay in Miami harbor. The ship was as tall as a 10-storey building. It dwarfed anything around it: trucks, containers, cars, people. And there was I, rolling my 34 kg suitcase along the pier with a computer bag dangling from my shoulder. I noticed a lot of activities. Boxes and cases were loaded and unloaded. Lorries were coming and going while forklifts were whizzing in between them. While I passed by the passenger luggage was stowed. One of the suitcases almost fell into the water; so much for safe baggage handling.

Finally, I found the gangway. I was confronted by a strict security guard: "You cannot come aboard. The ship has not been cleared yet." I declared my role as the new ship's doctor. That triggered some communication on a two-way radio between the security guard and his superior. I was made to wait and after a few minutes a man in a white uniform appeared. It was Dr. Stephen Moran, the senior ship's physician, who greeted me warmly. I boarded the ship and Stephen guided me to the mess, where we had a coffee and a little chat. It was a mixture between a welcome speech and a professional check-up. He asked questions such as: "Where did work before?" and "What is your professional background?"

M/S Victory

My baggage was safely stored in the ship's infirmary. Stephen was busy like the rest of the crew so he left me to my own devices. I walked freely all over the vessel. There was activity everywhere. This was the end and the beginning of a cruise at the same time. The total turnaround had to happen within a few hours. 3,000 passengers were leaving and 3,000 passengers arriving. Some crewmembers had left and some, like me, just joined the ship. All waste had to be disposed of and supplies restocked. The whole ship was cleaned and prepared for its new journey. I climbed onto the Panorama Deck, from where I had a great view over Miami. Well, I was about to go to sea.

The departure was an anti-climax. No waving good-bye, no music, no confetti. Well, there might have been, but I wouldn't know because I was stuck down below, in the ship's infirmary. While the ship sailed out of the harbor, I was treating patients with my colleague Stephen. We dealt with the usual general practice stuff: lost medication, stomach upsets, aches and pains. There was nothing new for me, except for a few drugs and the paperwork, which was strictly US-style.

At the end of our joint surgery (period of consultations) I went to my cabin. It consisted of a living area, a bedroom and a tiny bathroom. The two windows (actually called portholes) provided me with a view of open water stretching to the horizon. As I found out later, to have a view to the outside was quite a luxury for a crew member. The cabin was also equipped with a TV and a video player. There was also a computer with internet access. What more would I need? I decided to have "just a little lie-down" before the meeting with my colleagues in the crew bar. It was scheduled for 9 pm. At 9:30 pm I received a phone call: "Wern, where are you?" I had fallen asleep. "Never mind. We'll see you in the morning."

Thursday, 14th of February 2002
Onboard the M/S Victory, Caribbean Sea

First Steps as a Ship's Doctor
After four days at sea, I already had become a valued member of the Carnival team. And the leader of this team, Bob Dickinson, came onboard. He was the big cheese: CEO of Carnival Cruise Line (CCL). CCL had a fleet of 16 ships at the time, with five on order. Its workforce of around 16,000 employees looked after millions of passengers each year.

Me, Bob, Stephen & his wife Samantha

I met the big cheese in person. He was onboard the *M/S Victory* for just a few hours. The occasion was the presentation of an award to the crew. A big assembly gathered on the Lido Deck: the captain, all senior officers and a delegation from the ordinary crew. Bob bestowed an eagle made of glass to *M/S Victory* as it was on top of the performance tables. Handshakes and smiles followed. Afterwards, the crew was offered photo ops. Who wants a photo with Bob? Well, ok then. The ship's medical team gathered around him. First, we smiled and then we saw a flash. I think I still have a copy of this photo – somewhere. I found it! See above.

My walk had become broad, I wore a white uniform and I had become accustomed to living on a ship. It appeared that I had turned into a seaman. And, as such, one had to have the traditional gin and tonic – after duty of course. I had a few with the rest of the medical team, my colleague Stephen and the five nurses. While I enjoyed my drink, I listened to a lot of gossip. One rumor had it that a nurse on another ship had been sacked without notice. Apparently, her performance was not good enough. Well, hearing that made me think and I asked myself: *How long will I survive?* For the next day a helicopter evacuation drill was scheduled so I was obliged to read the handbook about that. It was a thick folder and I decided to make it my bedside reading

The ship became my hometown and the cabin my apartment. The town had a population of 4,200 inhabitants – more than some villages on shore have. This floating town had a lot to offer: restaurants, a gym, a large auditorium for dance performances, a disco, several bars, shops, a cinema, a hairdresser, many swimming pools and even a golf course. Well, the latter was actually just a cage with a simulation screen. By far the biggest area was occupied by the casino. I learnt later that this amusement was actually the main money-spinner for the cruise line – as well as the bars (BBB = booze brings bucks).

My cabin onboard the M/S Victory

One of the passengers had too much to drink that night. First, he shook violently and then he passed out – at 2 am in the morning. Guess which doctor had to attend to him? Dr. S. of course! I was the duty doctor that day. The on-calls were shared between Stephen and me. That meant being 24 hours on and then 24 hours off. Well, that night I had only the one customer. But I was tired the next day. Tiredness is the norm when working on ships, Karen told me. She was the nurse with whom I shared my first on-call. The duty nurse gets the requests for medical help first. She has to put up with a lot of crap and then calls the doctor if necessary. Karen was from New Zealand and was a friendly and helpful person. Jean was an elderly nurse, also from New Zealand. Unfortunately, she was absolutely useless and was sacked a few weeks after we set sail. Carmen was the lead nurse. She was from the US and absolutely in charge. She did things her way but knew pretty much everything. And then there was Amy form the UK. She was alright, but not particularly friendly. The fifth nurse was Samantha, the wife of Stephen, my colleague. She was totally unpretentious, competent and always friendly and helpful. Well, that was it – the medical team – a small but important department onboard the *M/S Victory* (my self-assessment). We worked together, ate together, and had fun together. There was so much togetherness during those days. But I wondered: *Will I fit in here?* And I thought: *Time will tell…*

From Ship to Shore

My first shore leave was in St. Juan, the capital of the island of Puerto Rico, and just one of the many isles in the Caribbean Sea. I was able to leave the ship following my afternoon surgery. By that time, it was already 7 pm. There was no customs or immigration to get through. The ships' security just had a quick look into my backpack at the gangway. A friendly "ping" resounded as I inserted my crew ID into the card reader and then I was free to leave the vessel.

It was already dark, and I had no idea where to go or what to do. I just followed the stream of people who walked along the illuminated harbour. It was a clear, warm night. I walked down the sea promenade together with hundreds of tourists. There was an endless array of hotels, bars and restaurants. I opted for a piña colada on a terrace where Caribbean music came from tiny loudspeakers. Then I made my way further down the esplanade towards the town. In the distance I could see the lights of a Hard Rock Café. Now, there was a chance for a decent beer. If you have been to one of the Hard Rock Cafés, then you have seen them all. They all look alike. Thus, as I entered it felt almost like going back to London or New York. This establishment in San Juan had the usual interior: guitars dangled from the wall, a large Jimmy Hendrix photo hung behind the bar and plenty of vinyl records were on display throughout the dining area.

However, I didn't come for the rock and roll stuff, but for a beer. And I wasn't disappointed. They even had German stuff such as Becks. But for a hell of a price! Still, it was worth it. It went down well, together with (in my opinion) good music – mainly from the 1980s. It was a slow night. Only a few tables were occupied, mainly by American tourists. I walked upstairs where more memorabilia was displayed. In a cabinet I discovered a contract for a book about a music band, The Doors. Then there were a few photos of Mick Jagger. A selection of vinyl records from Elvis Presley were hanging framed on the wall. I had another beer. I needed to speed up my drinking – only 20 minutes of my shore leave were left. I hurried back to the ship, together with a large crowd of crew and guests alike. The machine registered my arrival onboard with another "ping" and that was it – my first shore leave. Was it exciting? I was not so sure.

The island of St. Thomas, Caribbean

What happens if...(the helicopter comes)

The next day at 10:30 am I had to participate in the helicopter evacuation drill. It took place on the Lido Deck aft. "Aft" stands for the very back of the ship. Security cleared the deck for the exercise. Present were three sea officers, the nurses and doctors, as well as fire fighters and security. So many uniforms in one place drew the attention of passengers and an ever-increasing crowd began to watch our activities. The staff captain was responsible for the drill – he was not the real captain, but in charge of daily business onboard the ship; the real captain was called "the master of the vessel". Also present was the bosun. His job was to make sure that everything was "shipshape" on deck. There were so many positions onboard a vessel, most of which I had never heard of.

The actual execution of the exercise was down to the Safety Officer. There was no real action - just a lot of talk. The first step of a helicopter evacuation was to clear the deck for it. The helicopter would not land on the ship but just hover over the deck. The corpsman in the helicopter then lowers a stretcher. The patient is placed into it and then winched up to the helicopter. And off they go. It sounded easy enough. But we were also told about the dangers surrounding this procedure. The helicopter rotors create a huge downdraught. For that reason, all loose objects on deck must be secured otherwise they would fly around with potentially catastrophic effects. Additionally, we were instructed not to touch the line coming down from the helicopter as it may be electrically charged. Many more scary things were mentioned by the Safety Officer surrounding a helicopter evacuation. It sounded to me that an airlift is actually quite hazardous.

My role as the ship's doctor during this undertaking was comparatively easy: to make the decision on whether there needed to be an evacuation. The captain (sorry, master of the vessel) has the final say, of course. But it is very unlikely that he would overrule the decision of a ship's doctor. That's because the doctor is the only person on board with medical expertise. Once the captain (master) has given the go-ahead it would be up to the doctor to organize the evacuation. He (or she) would have to communicate with the coastguard and also with the HQ in Miami, because CCL liked to know what was happening on their vessels. The ship's doctor would then have to get the patient ready for the airlift, and, and, and... It appeared that the doctor would be actually very busy person in that kind of situation. Eventually, the Safety Officer finished his little speech by asking if anyone had any questions. But nobody did. That was the end of the drill.

Becoming a Member of the "Carnival Family"

After the drill, I had lunch on the open-air section of the Lido Deck. Sitting amongst the passengers in a white uniform wearing a "doctor" name tag could be hazardous. It was often seen as an invitation for guests to ask silly questions. It could be harmless remarks such as "How is it going, Doc?" or simple questions like "Where is the purser's office?" But by far the worst was a question beginning with the line: "I have this pain..." However, that day I was able to enjoy my food in peace. The sun was out, and a gentle breeze made the air cool and fresh. The ship rocked gently from side to side while it ploughed its way through the deep blue sea. It was like being in a TV ad. But it was reality.

That afternoon I was scheduled to attend a training course. The venue was pleasant enough: the Red and Black Bar. No drinks but coffee and cookies were served. All the "newbies" (new crew members) had to attend. Consequently, I met crew from different departments: a cook, barmaids, cabin stewards, engineers and an accountant. We were a group of 40 people or so. The topic of the course was "Crowd Management". We were put through a practical exercise. Three of the participants were the crew and the rest of us were guests (passengers). The task of the crew members was to guide the guests to the muster station, the part of the ship where the passengers have to go in case of an emergency or disaster. Some of the people who played the guests had to be unruly and the crew members had the task of dealing with them – hence the topic of the course. The exercise ended in a complete chaos, highlighting the need for the lesson. Afterwards we were shown a video on how it should be done properly, including some techniques on how to calm down unruly passengers.

One of the many little guys who keep the ship afloat,
Ship's Casino

The last part of the course was a lecture about safety rules. We were instructed what to do in case of fire or when someone falls overboard. Each crewmember had different tasks in these circumstances. It turned out that the doctor had to report to the infirmary whatever happens onboard the ship. And, yes, I had a place in a life raft. I was allocated a seat in boat number 64. It was to be found "forward starboard". That is a seaman's term, meaning in front of the ship, on the right-hand side. The training ended with a written test. Not a great challenge for me. But some crewmembers were struggling due to their limited English skills. But with some coaching from the instructors, everybody passed somehow. At the end, all of us received a small flashlight and a colorful certificate.

The day ended in Stephen's cabin, where I had a few drinks with him, his wife and the senior nurse, Carmen. It was a relaxed atmosphere and I listened to inside stories about the "Carnival Family". Working for an American company was very different from serving the NHS (National Health Service) in the UK. For a start a ship's doctor provides a service for customers (the passengers, called guests) and he or she also has to deal with the employees (the ship's crew) who came from all corners of the world. Actually, most of the crewmembers came from relatively poor countries such as India or Indonesia and they worked very hard for their money. Their shifts were usually 10 to 15 hours long and they were contracted to work every day for up to six months! Their wages were (compared to Europe or the US) quite low. A cook, for example, earned around US $700 per month. Food and accommodation were free, though. Crewmembers also enjoyed free medical care (with some limitations), which was a big plus for many of them. So, overall, it was probably not a bad deal for most of them to work on a cruise ship. Even though their working and living conditions were probably not in line with European standards. But they were (like me then) part of "Carnival Family".

Learning what to do (and what not to do)

I was looking out the window of my room at the Marriott Hotel in Tampa, Florida. It was raining like hell, but still warm. I had a few hours to kill until signing on to my ship, the *M/S Jubilee* (M/S stands for Motor Ship). So, I had some time to reflect on the past two weeks. On Sunday, 17 February, my seven-day introduction journey on the *M/S Victory* had ended at Miami harbour. After signing off I travelled straight to the hotel and being dead tired, I just collapsed onto the bed for a long, long sleep.

The next day I had to attend medical classes at the UM (University of Miami). Most of the participants were paramedics from the FD (Fire Department). About a group of 15 of us learned how to deal with medical emergencies by attending the ACLS (Advanced Cardiac Life Support) course. During a break I had a chat with the guys from the fire brigade. Their scope of work in the US appeared to be quite different from what is done in Europe. In America paramedics can give all kind of drugs, including narcotics. This is done according to protocols. However, these protocols were set by the medical director of each fire station so there was quite a bit of variety in what should be done in specific circumstances. US paramedics perform all sorts of procedural tasks like inserting IV (intra-venous) lines or intubating patients. It turned out that they were really good at it, which was no wonder – they did this sort of thing almost every day. There were also three doctors on the course so I was not alone. One was working in an AIDS clinic, another was involved in sleep studies and the third one was a radiologist. We discussed our different health systems (US vs. NHS in England), but came to the same conclusion: hospitals and doctors often work beyond capacity. And the whole system becomes impossible to fund. But somehow the show goes on.

Downtown Miami

During a lunch break I heard an interesting story from one of the firemen. Paramedics had been called to an emergency and were confronted with a lifeless patient. All efforts to revive the patient failed so they contacted an ER (Emergency Room) doctor at the hospital for advice. He agreed to cease all efforts. Now the crew was stuck with a dead body as hospitals don't accept deceased patients and the public morgue is only for the police department. Well, they had to dispose of the body somehow. Their solution was to drive to the home of the deceased and put him into bed there. Then they asked the relatives to call a funeral director to deal with the dead body. That was of course NOT the appropriate action to take. And the next day this story was in all newspapers.

The ACLS course was quite intense. It lasted for two days with lectures in the morning and hands-on exercises in the afternoon. But the organizers made it quite fun. They loosened up the teaching with funny videos, jokes and quizzes. And everything we had to learn was broken down into small bits, easy to remember. Well, I suppose that was the American style of teaching. Still, I learned a lot and noticed that a great many things were done quite differently on this side of the Atlantic. The course ended with a multiple choice test. I got 92 percent of the questions right with 84 percent required for a pass. I received yet another certificate I could hang onto the wall.

TV on, Olympics on

After that effort, I had some leisure time. I didn't do much for a few days – mainly watching TV as the Winter Olympics were on. The constant advertising breaks were a pain in the butt, but I still enjoyed following some of the competitions. The women's figure skating was extensively covered. I think it was because the American women's team was destined to get medals. Michele Kwan was one of them. She was an experienced athlete and destined to win gold. Her victory could only be spoiled by the Russian competitor: Irina Slutskaya – or so the commentators thought. But at the end another American won gold: Sarah Hughes. She was just 16 years old and that showed. Not during her performance on the ice, but throughout the TV interviews thereafter. She was very immature and I found it painful to listen to her babble. It seemed that she didn't comprehend what had just happened to her: getting fame – and money. Well, the latter will come in a while after the advertising contracts are signed (Michele Kwan promoted Chevrolet cars for example). But how long will the fame last for? Who won gold in figure skating in 1998? I don't know! Do you?

After two days of rest, I had to fly from Miami to Tampa, which is on the other side of Florida. It's just a quick trip by plane – barely an hour's flight. Hardly worth going through all the trouble of the security checks, which I really hate. The flight itself was extremely bumpy. It was so bad that the flight attendances stopped serving drinks. Once I arrived at the other end, I took a taxi to the hotel. There I indulged in watching the TV stretched out on the bed and I ordered some food from room service, so everything was set for a good night. I watched the Olympics (again) and came across a game of (ice) hockey: USA vs. Russia. It seemed to be THE game, according to the hype surrounding it. At the end the US team won 3:2, holding the score by just a thin thread. The next game for the US team would be against Canada – for gold!

Wednesday, 27th February 2002
Caribbean Sea

The Grand Tour on Grand Cayman

It was the last night of my hand-over cruise on the *M/S Jubilee*. That evening, I downloaded some photos for my doctor colleague, Manuela Jakobi from the farewell party. The next day we were due to arrive in Tampa, Florida, our home port. Upon arrival she was due to leave the ship and I was meant to stay. From then onwards I was destined to fly solo, so to speak.

A nice journey had come to an end and I had the luxury of being able to share the burden of the doctor's duties with Manuela. Akin to me, she had gained her medical degree in Germany and then had trained in the UK to become a GP. Throughout our joint journey she had been pleasant and supportive, although a bit chaotic at times. That cruise was her last voyage; her six months on the *Jubilee* came to an end and my six months were about to begin.

A port of call during that particular cruise were the Cayman Islands. Coral reefs prevent larger vessels from docking at the harbor pier. For that reason, cruise ships had to anchor off the shoreline and passengers were brought to the island by small boats. The only chance to see the Cayman Islands was during the handover journey. Regulations demand that a doctor has to be onboard a cruise ship at all times. The only exception is when the vessel is in port, because then an ambulance can be called for medical emergencies. But since the *Jubilee* had to anchor *off* the Cayman Islands, a physician had to be on board. Fortunately, during the hand-over cruise Manuela was able cover for me so I took the tender onshore. The *Jubilee* was not the only vessel visiting the Cayman Islands that day and the surrounding waters were full of other cruise ships.

George Town, Grand Cayman

After a wobbly transfer, I set foot on Grand Cayman, the largest island in the archipelago. My first steps took me along the promenade near the quay. I was determined to make the best out of this outing. But what I was faced with was just a gigantic shopping area with loads of bars and restaurants scattered in between. Jewelry seemed to be the big seller there. I had booked the "Grand Cayman Tour", a two-hour bus excursion organized for passengers but free of charge for me as a crew member.

Tourist Trap, Grand Cayman

The first stop was at a rum cake shop. Our bus was just one of many in the car park – it was tourism gone mad. I had to queue to get into the shop only to join another line to sample the cake. And then I had to queue again to get a cake and to pay for it. But, hey, there was a positive surprise at the cashier: I was entitled to a 20 percent discount as a member of a ship's crew. I stuffed the cake into my backpack and climbed back onto the bus. While we were leaving George Town, the capital of the Cayman Islands, the tour guide told us about the origin of its name. It was derived from King George III, who reigned from 1760 to 1820. Legend has it that he promised not to raise any taxes on the Cayman Islands while he was the ruler of the British Empire. Whether that is true or not, the Cayman Islands still don't have any direct taxes such as income or capital gains tax to this day.

Instead, the government opted for other sources of revenue such as import duties and levies on property. The Cayman Islands are a BOT (British Overseas Territory), which means they are still under the jurisdiction of the United Kingdom, without being actually part of it. A complicated political construct which stems from the fact that the Cayman Islands were British colonies but decided not to become independent. So, they are *a kind of* British. That explained why the bus was driving on the left – for me the wrong side of the road. According to the tour guide, the islands had a population of 35,000 citizens plus 6,000 permanent residents at the time of my visit. The wealth on the Caymans was described as high and the crime rate as low. And, yes, the tour guide mentioned the 300 banks registered on this little island, shuffling around billions of dollars. (Better not to know whose money they handle).

The tour bus rolled along the west coast of Grand Cayman. We were allowed to leave the bus for a few minutes to see the famous Seven Mile Beach. There, the governor of the Cayman Islands has his residence. The governor at the time was Peter Smith. I don't know how busy he was during his posting. Part of his job was to represent the Queen of England – and to enjoy a private strip of the magnificent beach, which I had a chance to look at.

Seven Mile Beach, Grand Cayman

The next stop was hell – well, not quite. It was just a black limestone formation of a size similar to a football pitch. According to a sign next to it, its name had come from a remark of a British Commissioner who once visited the island. No date was given as to when that happened, but apparently he exclaimed: "My God, this must be what hell looks like". When I was there, it was a well-developed tourist site with shops galore. Tourist could buy mugs, posters, and T-shirts stating "I have been to hell". Personally, I couldn't agree more. But for different reasons; that place was a horrible tourist trap.

At the turtle farm, Grand Cayman

Our final destination was a turtle farm in the northwest corner of the island, where about 7,000 turtles were held in grey concrete basins. The farm raised turtles for their meat which was made available to restaurants and gourmet shops. The guide, who showed the bus group around the farm, claimed that the farm also had some conservation purposes. According to him, hundreds of turtles are released into the ocean each year to maintain a natural stock. However, I felt sorry for the turtles which had to live in their hundreds in dark concrete tanks. And, worse, some of them became photo models. The guide took two out of the reservoir and handed them to the visitors, who could take pictures of and with them. So, the poor creatures went from hand to hand to be photographed by John, Mary, Tom, Harry… and, and, and. I couldn't watch it any longer and walked away from it all.

A few minutes later, I was sitting in the bus again. As we rolled slowly back towards George Town. I was amazed to see a traffic jam on this little island. But in a way it was not surprising. According to our guide the island had more cars than people.

Once back at the pier in George Town I had to queue with a huge crowd which was waiting for the transfer to the cruise ship by tender boats. The wait was sweetened by a band playing Caribbean rhythms but that didn't improved my mood. It was hot, I was tired, and I knew that I will be on duty again as soon as I was back onboard.

A Goodbye with a big Hat (and Head)
The remaining part of "handover-cruise" was a mixture of stress and fun. First, let's talk about the good part of the journey. We all (the medical department) went to a restaurant in Cozumel, Mexico. There we had a kind of goodbye dinner for Manuela, who was due to leave the ship at the end of the cruise. We had nachos, champagne and lots of tequila. The next morning my head felt bigger than the sombrero I had worn that night.

Mexican farewell party

On the journey back to Tampa we had less fun. A passenger developed severe heart problems. She was very sick and needed to be evacuated, but the weather was bad and the winds were too strong for a helicopter evacuation. So, we had to care for this lady for the rest of the journey. However, the ship steamed at full speed towards Tampa and we managed to arrive a few hours early. Upon arrival an ambulance was already waiting at the quayside to bring the patient to the hospital. Just half an hour later we had to attend to another passenger who had suffered a stroke. I began to wonder, whether my next six months would be always like this.

A tough Call

My first solo cruise had an inauspicious start. I managed to delay the departure of the vessel for almost an hour. Finally, I made my way to the bridge to sign the register, so the ship could leave the harbor. But let start at the beginning.

Just a few hours earlier, I had hugged my doctor colleague Manuela goodbye. From that moment on I was the only doctor onboard. That morning I decided to get familiar with the "Jube". I wandered along the decks from aft to midship and then forward on the starboard side. Afterwards walked back on the port side. (That is ships' speak. It means that I walked from the back to the middle of the ship, then to the front of it on the right side. And then I took my way back on the left side.) I also inspected "my" lifeboat. It had the number eight. I needed to know where to go if I was faced with a "Titanic situation" onboard this ship.

M/S Jubilee

After lunch I rearranged the doctor's consulting room to my liking. I thought I need to be comfortable there, as it was destined to be my workplace for the next six months. Afterwards, I retired to my cabin to have a little rest but my respite didn't last long. Just 20 minutes later I was called by security at the gangway. "The passenger you were waiting for is here," I was told. Indeed, I had asked them to call me when Mr. Smith (let's call him by that name) arrived. His doctor had contacted Carnival, warning us that he was not fit to go onto a cruise, hence I wanted to see him before he could come onboard. I met the passenger (pardon, *guest*) in front of the departure terminal. He didn't look too healthy, sitting in a wheelchair with a grey face. His wife was with him. What now? I had to assess him to determine whether he was fit to travel but I couldn't do that on the street. So I decided to get him into the ship's infirmary. After I had examined him there, I deduced that he had a serious case of COPD (= having serious problems to breathe).

His doctor was right to conclude that this gentleman was not fit to travel. Mr. Smith was a medical time bomb who could turn into an emergency at any minute. I got in touch with the HQ in Miami, asking what should be done. "Well, you may have to deny him sailing with you, but the decision is yours. You are the doctor on the ground there," was the answer.

That was not really helpful. I discussed the situation with the second officer, who then called the captain (well, "master of the vessel"). He asked what the likelihood was that the passenger would need to be evacuated from the ship. That was difficult to predict. He could be alright, but equally it could turn into a major medical disaster. The captain wanted an answer there and then. At that moment I started to sweat. Adrenalin was rushing through my veins and I felt a little dizzy for a moment. But then I made a clear decision: "Yes, Mr. Smith carries a great medical risk. If he falls ill the ship may have to be diverted. The situation might even require a helicopter evacuation. So, Mr. Smith has to disembark."

M/S Jubilee, full steam ahead

A lot of Talk - for Nothing
The chief purser (head of administration) was accordingly informed. Note: she was also the captain's wife. "Leave it to me," were her words. I walked up to the bridge and waited for the message that Mr. Smith had left the vessel. After that I would be able to sign the register, stating that all was well and the medical department was ready to sail. Instead of getting the good news however, a call came to summon me to the purser's office. There a little group was waiting for me: Monica, the chief purser, Fred the hotel director (who was in charge of all issues concerning passengers), as well as the guest in question and his wife. The latter two were not in a good mood. They were actually extremely angry. And it was me who got the heat. "Doc, why did you change your mind?" I was asked. I explained to them that I didn't, I just allowed them to come onboard for a medical evaluation. And I told them that it was too dangerous for Mr. Smith to travel onboard a cruise ship. "Your own doctor thinks so," I emphasized. "No, he does not," argued the wife. "Well, we received a fax to that effect," I replied. "That cannot be correct," disputed the wife. She got her cell phone (UK speak: mobile phone) out and tried to talk to their family doctor. Alas, he was not available. What followed was a heated debate. Nasty words came out of the guests' mouths. But I was not in the position to pay them back. I had to put on the "Carnival Smile" and stay polite. I was firm with my argument but Mr. Smith and his wife were adamant that they would stay. So, what were the options? To get security to throw them out by force? Not good for PR. So, they stayed. And we left the harbor with them onboard – with a delay of almost an hour. For nothing.

Monday, 4th of March 2002
Tampa, Florida, USA

Life as a Ship's Doctor
Another "Tampa Day", indicating the ship was docked at its homeport Tampa, Florida. A Tampa Day was always a more relaxed day for me. No regular surgeries to run, only one hour of consultations in the evening. It was a kind of a day off. Accordingly, I was free to leave the ship. However, I couldn't be bothered to go on shore that day. First of all, I had to catch up with sleep and therefore had a lie-in. Secondly, I wanted to settle into my new quarters onboard. They consisted of a living room with a TV and a computer, a bathroom with a bathtub and

shower, a bedroom with a double bed, and a cloakroom for my uniform and luggage. The bedroom and living room had portholes (windows in ship's speak). Considering that space on a ship is a precious commodity, my accommodation was quite luxurious. A few weeks later I saw the living quarters of an "ordinary" crewmember. It consisted of a windowless room deep down in the bowels of the ship with four bunk beds and a shared bathroom down the corridor.

Doctor onboard

The *Jubilee* was built in 1986 as (what Carnival called) a "Holiday Class" vessel. Ships of that class were the first that Carnival built from scratch. They carried about 1,500 passengers and around 700 crewmembers. The *Victory*, on which I sailed just a few weeks earlier, was much bigger. It belonged to the "Destiny Class". Vessels of that class were able to accommodate 2,700 passengers and 1,100 crewmembers. Because of its size the *Victory* had two doctors, whereas the smaller *Jubilee* had only one doctor serving onboard.

So, what was it like to be a ship's doctor? What people usually imagine is this: wearing a fancy white uniform, being an important senior officer, walking along a sunny deck, chatting with passengers, attending cocktail parties and eating at the captain's table. Well, all of that is true to some degree. But what is not seen by most was the bloody hard work behind those scenes. For instance, the sick patient I had to look after for 48 hours non-stop, the helicopter evacuation at 3 am in the morning and the strain of being permanently on duty. Any medical problem onboard the ship was my problem. And living on a floating vessel was very different from living in a home. It was not possible to pop out to see a friend down the road. Everything I did on board was closely watched by guests and fellow crewmembers alike. And there were no weekends or days off. The only break I got from work were the few hours when the ship was in its home port Tampa.

A day of Ship's Doctor's life
Let me describe a typical day onboard the *M/S Jubilee*. At 6:30 am or so, I dragged myself out of bed. Around 7:00 am I managed to have my breakfast in the officers' or staff mess. The latter was frequented by middle ranks and the food was served as a buffet, but the dishes were cleared by waitresses. Whereas in the officers' mess a full waitress service was available and the interior was a bit more fancy. The third-class dining was the crew mess, which was open to all crew members. There you had to get your food from a counter and the dishes had to be handed over to the cleaners after the meal. The facilities in that mess consisted of bare tables and simple seats. Personally, I preferred the staff mess because the food was instantly available and I was able to avoid my fellow senior officers, who often talked a lot of rubbish.

After breakfast I would make my way to the infirmary. My workplace was a small but adequate place with just a counter (and a nurse behind it), my consulting room and a treatment room. I started to see patients at 8:00 am. My "customers" were passengers and crew alike. The typical passenger came with a cold and cough and with an attitude problem. "I want..." was what I heard from them a lot. Their mind set was: "I pay for this consultation, so I get what I want" (which were mainly antibiotics or other medication). But that was not how I practiced medicine. Medication has to be prescribed according to a patient's needs not for their convenience. The crew was another matter. They were a very diverse lot, coming pretty much from all corners of the world. That meant I had to deal with very different attitudes towards health. As they were working long hours without much of a break, many of the crew's troubles were occupational health issues. But most of the crewmembers were young and fit. And if they were not, then Carnival wouldn't have hired them in the first place.

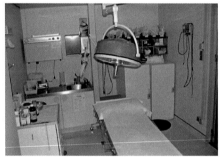

Ship's infirmary, M/S Jubilee

Around 11:00 am the waiting area became empty and I could attend to the admin side of my job. Much of my time was spent to read and sending e-mails. Messages were sent within the ship, ship to ship, ship to shore, and shore to ship. A lot of communication came towards me. As a head of the medical department, I was copied on all sorts of messages. Some were useful, but most of them went straight into the recycle bin. But there was still actual paperwork to attend to. A lot of forms had to be completed and many reports were written. All of this kept me amused for hours.

High Noon
At 12:00 noon I often had to attend a meeting. Once per journey the official captain's meeting took place at that time. All department heads then sat in the spacious captain's cabin, slurping coffee and listening to the latest problems onboard the ship. Once I had survived this kind of get-together, it was finally time for my lunch. On occasions one of my fellow officers or the nurse on duty joined me for a meal. My favorite lunch spot was the Lido Deck, where food of all kinds was available for guests and officers alike. When lunching with a companion, the chance to exchange the latest gossip arose. And there was plenty of that going around the ship!

Following lunch, I did what Winston Churchill used to do – having a little nap. Refreshed and with renewed energy, I was able to write this diary or to send e-mails and messages to friends and family back home. Afterwards I had to return to my place of duty, the infirmary. The afternoon surgery started at 3 pm and officially lasted until 6 pm, but often didn't finish before 7 pm or even later. You cannot send patients away when you are the only doctor around for hundreds of (sea) miles.

The evenings were often filled with official engagements like a dinner at the captain's table or the "Penguin Parade". But I will talk about that later. If I was free after work, I favored the crew bar for relaxation. There I could have a chat and a drink with my fellow crewmembers without the risk of being hassled by a guest. Every so often (when I was really tired) I just went to my cabin, ordered food from room service and watched television. (My absolute favorite at the time was *Law and Order* – an American crime series.)

Doctor's cabin, M/S Jubilee

Well, that it! I just described a typical day of my life as a ship's doctor. But most days were NOT typical. Very often something unexpected happened, good and bad. However, I enjoyed the excitement of being in unchartered waters and relishing the occasional adrenalin rush. But I wondered whether that would last for the whole six months of my contract.

Thursday, 7ᵗʰ of March 2002
Crew Bar, M/S Jubilee

A Society of Classes
The Crew Bar was a small but cozy place, located near the bow (front) of the ship. It was an egalitarian place: all were equal in there. It didn't matter how many stripes you had on your uniform or what your function was on the ship. In there the chief engineer and cleaner were the same: just patrons of the bar.

Nevertheless, the ship's world outside the Crew Bar was a different matter – divided into three classes. The lower class consisted largely of un- or low-skilled workers such as cleaners, deckhands, waiters, cooks and the like. They lived on the lower decks in four- to six-bed cabins with shared bathrooms and had to eat in the crew mess. Dancers, casino staff, hairdressers, shop assistants and crewmembers with a similar function made up the middle class. They had their own mess (staff mess), where they took their meals and had to share their cabin with just one other person. Members of the upper class were the ship's officers. That included all the sea officers, the ship's purser, hotel director, food and beverage manager, the housekeeping manager (supervising the cabin stewards and cleaners) and, of course, the ship's doctor. We, the "upper crust", had our own cabins and dined in the officers' mess or (on occasion) at the captain's table. Of course, officers could choose to "go lower", which I frequently did by eating in the staff mess. I visited the crew mess only once for experience. Too many eyes were fixated on me during my meal there. And I think the crewmembers were uncomfortable themselves with having an officer in their world.

Having fun in the Crew Bar

The crew came from all parts of the world – the ship was a kind of United Nations. Yet, we were all able to work (and laugh) together. Even though, the community was also subject to constant changes. Each time we docked at our home port, Tampa, crewmembers signed on or off. Their contract to work onboard a ship was sometimes as long as eight or nine months, but typically ran between four and six months. Carnival didn't pay them between contracts but covered the cost of travel and provided medical care whilst onboard (which was largely provided by me as the ship's doctor).

A Sanctuary for Staff
Thankfully, no guests were allowed in the Crew Bar, which made that place an area of refuge. Just being away from the demands of guests was a holiday in itself – even if it was just for an hour or two. Business was slow when I entered the bar that evening as it was just 9 pm. I ordered my favorite drink: a bottle of Corona beer with a piece of lime sticking out of the bottle neck. Since the bartender wasn't busy, I had the chance to have a little a chat with him. David was a fountain of knowledge (and gossip) as he knew almost every member of staff on the ship. As he got busy with other customers, I looked around to see who else was coming in to have a break.

Fancy a game of darts?
Crew Bar, M/S Jubilee

All the crewmembers were easily identifiable given that all members of staff were nicely labeled with a name tag on their shirt. Mine said: "Dr. Werner Schomburg – Ship's Physician, Germany". I peeked at the label of the girl next to me which stated: "Hedvika – Purser, Czech. Republic". I initiated a conversation with her by asking the usual questions between crewmembers: Are you on your first contract? Which ships have you worked on? How long have you worked for Carnival? When does your contract end? The topic of conversation then went to what we did on the ship. Hedvika worked at the information desk. Her job was to listen to all the complaints and demands from the guests. (John, my lead nurse always wondered why the passengers were called guests. "I didn't invite them", he always said.) Anyway, we then discovered that we both had lived in England for a while. She had studied business in London, while I had worked as a junior doctor in the North of England. The conversation flowed like a river and we lost track of the time. Suddenly, the lights were dimmed, signaling that the bar was about to be closed. It was 2 am and time to go to sleep.

Friday, 8th of March 2002
Cozumel, Mexico

Meet the (A) Team
The bar near the pier in Cozumel, Mexico was called "Fat Tuesday" – don't ask me why. I think it has to do something with the carnival celebrations. I was sitting on the veranda having a piña colada with the view towards the "Jube". The ship looked really good – from the outside. Having that view meant I was not on it and therefore off duty.

Ships' Terminal, Cozumel, Mexico

While I relaxed at the Fat Tuesday, I pondered about my new work situation. The medical department was the smallest department onboard the *Jubilee*. It consisted of just three nurses and me. Still, by definition, I was a department head with all the advantages and disadvantages attached to this position. I had the privilege of dining at the captain's table and occupied a large cabin. The downside was that I had to attend almost every meeting which took place on the ship. Most of them were a waste of time. I often wondered how the medical department could help to fix some trouble in the engine room or what we could do about the falling revenue from the casino and bars. However, I was blessed with having a good team around me. Let me introduce them to you: There was Sonia, a nurse from Scotland with work experience in Saudi Arabia; she was a very social person and well connected. Almost everybody on board knew her and she knew everybody. If I wanted to get something done, I never filled out a request form, I just asked her, and she knew somebody who knew somebody who could to the job. The second nurse was Linda; she was from Texas, USA, an experienced ER nurse. She was very efficient and capable of carrying out any medical procedure such as sticking needles into patients.

Linda spoke Spanish fluently and this enabled her to deal easily with all the Hispanics, whether they were crewmembers or passengers. She was not what one would call an outgoing person, more a quiet one, keeping mainly to herself. And then there was John, the lead nurse. He was happily and openly gay. Why he was so popular with the girls, I never found out. Maybe they just felt safe with him, being confident that he wouldn't pursue a sexual relationship. John had "done the ships" for two years when I met him. As a lead nurse he earned a little bit more money (50 cents per hour extra) but had much more responsibility and endless paperwork. I noticed that he was often tired. It seemed that he had enough of living afloat. He was scheduled to sign off in five weeks. His plan was to quit the ships for good and to return to his hometown, Liverpool in England. Well, that's it! You just met the little team I was working with at the time.

The infirmary team (from the left):
Doctor, Linda, Sonia, Dr. Manuela, John

The Absence of Fun
My time at the Fat Tuesday had come to an end and I had to return to the ship. The current "Run" (as crewmembers refer to a journey) was different. It was a Bible cruise. The whole ship was chartered by Bible-bashers under the lead of the Pastor Charles Stanley. The tickets for that cruise were more expensive than regular tickets with an add-on of US $ 300, sold by church organizations. Well, Charles Stanley was a celebrity, a well-known pastor of the Baptist Church, whose sermons were televised all over the US. He had published many books about Christianity. Having a journey with him was worth the extra money for many – the cruise was sold out.

The whole cruise was centered around religious activities, mainly preaching and praying. There were Bible study groups and special pastoral care was available. Nonetheless, the absence of fun was striking. The casino and the discotheque were closed and there were no dance shows. The bars sold only coke and juices. Even the swimming pools were emptied. All youth on the ship had a strict curfew of 10 pm. The onboard TV programming was tightly controlled. The movie *One Fine Day* with George Clooney was found to be unsuitable by the organizers. Not exactly a movie loaded with sex or violence. Still, it was axed during the second day of the cruise. How narrow-minded can one get?

The Messiah sells
One evening I took a stroll along the Promenade Deck after a hard day's work. This deck was normally packed with people, music and laughter. That night there was nothing but dead silence. Only a few passengers were about; there was some comings and goings from the casino

but people weren't going there to gamble. The area was converted to a shopping mall. On the roulette and black jack tables, Bibles were on sale. One could choose from an array of different editions. The holy book was available as paperback, hardback or in leather, with or without illustrations. Also, CDs with recordings of religious music, gospels and prayers were available. And, of course, all sorts of Stanley memorabilia could be found: his books, CDs of his speeches and videos of his preaching.

Charles Stanley (Google Images)

As I looked around the many vendor stalls, I was approached by an elderly man. He praised Stanley as if the guy was a messiah. With trembling hands, he presented a book from the man himself to me, saying that it contained all that is needed to gain happiness. That man sounded absolutely genuine to me. As a matter of fact, I think he was a true believer. But I also think he was deceived. This cruise and all the merchandising had only one purpose: to make money. And he was just one of the many little guys who contributed to this multimillion-dollar business. I truly felt sorry for him.

Ships' layout, M/S Jubilee

As the ship started to move, I stepped out onto the open deck to watch the lights of Cozumel disappearing in the distance. The *Jubilee* was underway again to its home port in Tampa. A lady, standing at the railing next to me, drew me into conversation. She told me a tale about her dull life filled with religious passion. And then she made a confession: She had sinned (!). I was bracing myself for a juicy story. But all she had done was to have a piña colada in a bar in Cozumel. (Oh, my God!!) Another passenger, whom I spoke with a little later that evening, was a bit more down to earth. She realized that she likes cruising and wanted to come back – for a REAL cruise.

Walking through the "Window"

It had been almost 10 days since I had taken charge of medical department onboard the *Jubilee*. During that time my feet had touched dry land only in Cozumel for a short stint. Sonia, the nurse, told me that I have to leave the ship more often in order to stay sane. So, that morning at 8 am, I lingered at the gangway, waiting for a "window" to open. A "window" was a time period during which crewmembers were allowed to go ashore. It usually opened early in the morning for about 2–3 minutes and then again around 10:30 am. The actual times depended on the immigration officers. They were pretty busy guys upon arrival of a cruise ship. All non-US guests and all crew members signing on (starting) or singing off (finished their contracted time on the ship) had to be cleared by immigration. Everybody concerned congregated in one of the larger spaces onboard, traditionally the disco, where they were processed by immigration officers. And it was one of these officers who gave the go-ahead for the opening of the window. Fred, the purser, oversaw of the clearing process and he frequently persuaded the officials to open the window for the crew – good lad!

Downtown Tampa

After a 15-minute wait, the "window" opened and Sonia and I could finally escape the ship. It was a fine day with bright sunshine and balmy temperatures. We walked from the quayside towards the downtown area of Tampa. As it was an early Saturday morning, so not many people or cars were about. The city had the appearance of a ghost town as we strolled along empty streets and passed deserted office buildings. It was a strange feeling to have a rock-solid surface under my feet again. At times I sensed that the pavement was swaying under my feet – an illusion after just 10 days onboard a ship. I wondered how a (real) seaman must feel when he walks on firm ground after many weeks at sea. I thoroughly enjoyed that early morning walk. For the first time in days, I had escaped the confinement of the ship, being able to march for miles (if I wanted) without being forced to go in circles.

The purpose of the outing was also to get some shopping done. I wondered whether I could get hold of a German newspaper or magazine. Onboard the ship only American television was broadcasted. US TV stations aired mainly soap operas and talk shows. The news bulletins were brief and mainly about the American President or where and when somebody had been killed. Then a bit of sports news and the weather and that was it! Hardly anything was reported of what took place outside the US. Well, the internet gave me some information about events that occurred around the world, but I was eager to learn what is happening back home in more detail.

Life on Shore

Before Sonia and I went onto a shopping spree we dropped into the Hyatt Hotel to have a coffee. We chose a table near the lobby fountain. The pleasant sound of falling water had a soothing effect on me after all that professional stress during the past week. With the coffee we had what the Americans call a "continental" breakfast: croissants, butter and jam.

The topic of our conversation was a dirty thing: money. Sonia told me that we were paid onboard the ship every fortnight in cash. I would get quite a few "greenbacks" (slang for dollars) every two weeks. The question arose: What to do with all that cash? Sonia had decided to wire the money to her home country, the UK. However, she told me that some crew members had opened bank accounts in the US to keep their wages money there. I considered opting for the latter, but I was not willing to pay any US taxes on my hard-earned dollars.

Walmart in Tampa, Florida, USA

After our little breakfast it was time to make a move. We grabbed a taxi which took us to our next stop: a huge Walmart store. The prices were low, but so was the quality of the stuff sold there. Also low were the wages Walmart paid its employees. I had read an article (I think it was in *The New York Times*) just a few weeks earlier about the so-called "Mc Jobs". These were jobs for workers with little or no skills which came with very diminutive wages. Some employees needed to hold two or even three of those positions in order to survive. Quite a few of these workers were so poor that they couldn't afford housing and had to live in their cars. So much for the "US job wonder".

"Here to help" was printed on the uniforms of the shop assistants at Walmart. I thought it was humiliating to be labeled like a poster. However, there was no need for me to bother any of them as the stuff I wanted was easy to find. I was just after basic necessities, such as shampoo, soap and sunscreen. The latter was a must-have when travelling in the Caribbean where the sun was so harsh that it was easy to get "sun poisoning" (the American expression for a sunburn). John, my lead nurse, hated the term, feeling that it implies that something happens merely by accident. In his opinion, it distracts from the fact that somebody was stupid enough to expose him- or herself to the sun without appropriate protection. "There is no such thing as sun poisoning," was one of John's classic lines. "This is not a medical emergency. I can see it from here," was another one when a guest demanded immediate treatment for a minor complaint. And if a guest asked him what a nurse consultation would cost, he might answer: "You already spent 10 dollars". That was John at his best.

Shop for the Ship

Another taxi ride took Sonia and me to a fancy shopping mall. Here the stores were far more glamorous than the Walmart box. Maybe it was that environment which got me into a shopping frenzy. I bought plenty of clothing, many videos and even a CD player, spending almost a thousand bucks (sorry, dollars). Still, I thought it was okay, as I didn't know when the next opportunity for shopping would arise.

International Plaza,
Tampa, Florida

After an exhausting shopping tour, it was time for lunch. We chose a fancy Italian restaurant just outside the mall. A giant parasol protected us against the harsh sun so we could enjoy the warmth of Florida without getting "sun poisoning". Munching a giant pizza, we discussed the joys and sorrows of working in the medical profession on a cruise ship. Sonia told me that she had worked for another cruise line before she came to Carnival. The doctor there worked on a commission basis. In order to maximize his income, he made the most of the facilities in the infirmary. Bloods were taken daily, x-rays were made frequently, and plenty of drugs were prescribed. That meant that the nurses were very busy without getting a cut from the profits generated. As a result, Sonia quit and was much happier on the "Jube". Carnival paid doctors and nurses a monthly salary, no matter how many (or few) patients they saw and no commission was paid. I think that was the right thing to do. Medicine and business don't mix well. No doctor is impartial about treatment if they have dollar signs in the back of their mind.

True Freedom, Tampa, Florida

Time flew and suddenly we realized that we had to go. We were due to be back on the ship by 3:15 pm to sail at 4 pm. A long (and expensive) taxi ride got us back to the cruise terminal. At its entrance it was not security but a heavily armed officer from the National

Guard, who asked for our ID. Another check took place on the pier and a third at the gangway. All these inspections were done in the wake of the events of 9/11. Once our bags were x-rayed and cleared, we were allowed to board the ship. I barely had the time for a quick shower and to change into my uniform before heading for the infirmary. Linda, who was on call that day had to remain onboard. She assured me that everything was ok. I then went up to the bridge to sign the logbook, confirming that the medical department was in good order and ready for yet another cruise.

Tuesday, 12th of March 2002
Cozumel, Mexico

A big Bang – and all was Silent

It was already late afternoon when the *M/S Jubilee* docked at the quay in Cozumel. The ship was scheduled to arrive in the early morning. I should have been on shore to enjoy a few hours of leisure. Instead, I stood on the bridge with binoculars, looking for an ambulance to arrive.

So, what happened? Let's go back to the night before. At around 11 pm I was called out for a passenger with abdominal pain. My diagnosis was gastric hemorrhage (bleeding from the stomach). I did what I could do for that man: poured fluids into him via his veins to keep his circulation stable. But what the patient needed was a blood transfusion and surgery to stop the bleeding. Unfortunately, neither could be provided onboard the ship, so the patient required urgent hospitalization. Our next port of call was Cozumel. I called the captain and asked him whether he could speed up the ship. He agreed to increase the speed to 22 knots. That means the ship would travel 22 nautical miles per hour. (1 nm = 1.12 land miles). Or to be less maritime: the speed was increased to 25 mph or roughly 40 km/h. It was not really a racing pace but would have brought us to Cozumel at around 7 am the next day.

Ship's engine room, M/S Jubilee

After a last check on the patient and final instructions for the guarding nurse I retired to my cabin for a few hours' sleep. At around 3 am I was woken up by a big bang, followed by some sort of rattling and then dead silence. *That is not good*, I thought. Normally I could hear the humming of the engine in the bedroom of my cabin. It was a kind of lullaby for me. But the engine had fallen silent. That meant that the ship had no propulsion and was just floating around somewhere in the Caribbean Sea. The phone next to my bed rang. The captain was on the line, confirming my suspicion. He told me that the ship had a major engine problem and that we would be arriving late in Cozumel.

The ship was still at sea at midmorning the next day. The engineering team had been able to get the engine somehow to work, but we were going rather slowly. The good news was that I was able to keep the patient alive. The first casualty in any emergency is information and it seemed nobody had any. Instead, rumors flew around the ship. What had happened? An explosion? A simple breakdown? Would the guests be flown home once we arrived in Mexico? Did we need to go into dry dock? Nobody seemed to know anything. In any case, that was not my concern. My worries revolved around the patient in the infirmary. It took another five hours until the ship finally arrived in Cozumel.

A Medical Procession

So, there I was, standing on the bridge of the *M/S Jubilee* with a pair of binoculars in my hands on the lookout for the ambulance. I checked with the captain whether the ambulance had been called, which he confirmed. After that I gave the purser a call, to ascertain its ETA. "It should be here any minute", was his answer. Finally, I saw a car with red flashing lights moving towards the pier – the ambulance. I rushed down to the infirmary to make the final preparations to disembark the patient. Within a few minutes the ship would dock.

While I was dealing with the final paperwork, talking to security, attending to the patient and speaking with his relatives onboard, the ambulance crew suddenly arrived in the infirmary. Thankfully, the accompanying doctor spoke English. I informed him about the medical situation and handed over all the relevant papers (medical report, charts, passport of the patient, etc.). The patient was transferred from the bed onto a stretcher and then wheeled through the lower decks towards the marshalling area (loading zone of the ship). The security guard led the way, followed by the patient on the stretcher with two paramedics and the wife. Behind them were the Mexican doctor, the purser, the lead nurse, and finally me. It was quite a crowd! It was a bumpy ride for the patient as it was quite difficult to get the stretcher through narrow passageways and the bulkhead doors (openings between compartments of a ship).

The Quay, Cozumel, Mexico

At last, we arrived at the crew gangway. Outside, on the pier we were greeted by quite a gathering – crewmembers and passengers alike. They had seen the ambulance and anticipated some excitement. I never understood the fascination in watching the accidents and misfortunes of other people. However, security guards were able to keep these people at bay and the patient was moved into the ambulance. The wife followed him with the luggage. John, the lead nurse, and I said goodbye to them and watched the ambulance as it whizzed down the quay with its siren wailing and red lights flashing. The spectator crowd dispersed once the "show" was over.

In the Bowels of the Ship

What is the difference between a 'wet' dock and a 'dry' dock? I didn't know that either until we had this engine trouble. Dry dock is a repair with the ship out of the water and wet dock is when it is still in the water. For the *Jubilee*, wet dock was prescribed. That meant to be tied up in Tampa for a few days.

But before going into wet dock in Tampa we had to return from Cozumel. The *Jubilee* left there at its usual scheduled time of 10 pm and was due to arrive in Tampa with a prospected delay of at least six hours. However, life onboard carried on as normal. The casino, the pool, bars, disco and restaurants were all open and the entertainment activities such as the dance shows went ahead as usual. But the ship was full of rumors and speculations of what actually had happened. Even the ship's command was unable to tell me what the real problem was. Eventually, I tried to get some information from the "horse's mouth" – the chief engineer.

The "trouble box"
(Pitch control)

But he was a busy and stressed man – unapproachable. So I went to his second in command: the staff chief engineer, a young man from Croatia. He was kind enough to let me crawl into the bowels of the ship to show me what the problem was. Actually, getting down into the engine room was quite an undertaking, climbing steep ladders and walking narrow passageways along smelly machinery. Finally, we stood in front of the part which had caused all the trouble and the engineer explained the situation to me. The ship had actually two engines; one on each side turns a propeller. It was the port (left side) engine which had failed. Well, actually not the engine as such but the pitch control of the propeller blades. With a fixed pitch it is very difficult to steer the ship and to reach a decent speed. The repair was expected to take a few days and the spare parts needed to be flown in from Sweden, where the ship was built.

Days of (paid) Fun

The ship arrived in Tampa after a seven-hour delay. The guests were allowed to stay onboard for an additional night as quite a few of them had missed their flights to get home. The next cruise was cancelled and the *Jubilee* stayed in Tampa harbor. No guests equaled no work for most of the crew but not for the guys from the engine department – they had to work very hard to fix the problem with the pitch control. And what about the ship's doctor? Well, I had just a daily "home port surgery" which lasted merely an hour from 5 to 6 pm. For the remaining hours I was free to go ashore to amuse myself. And I certainly did that! One evening I joined the ship's musicians, Mandy and Richard, as well as Sonia the nurse for a great night out. We went to an Irish pub and listened (and danced) to Irish folk music. The action was augmented by a lot of Guinness beer. After a few hours of sleep on the ship we went ashore again for a round of golf. And the best part was that all of us got paid during our spells of fun. We still got our salaries throughout the *Jubilee's* wet dock.

The Jubilee during Wet Dock

But nobody knew how long this sweet life would last. There were plenty of rumors, of course. Would the ship be ok for the next cruise? Would we be going into dry dock? On the third day of wet dock, the ship left the harbor (with the medical team onboard) to test the repaired engine at sea. On the fourth day the fun was over, and we took guests onboard for another cruise. Those four days must have cost the Carnival quite a bit of money in lost revenues and the cost to repair the engine was probably quite substantial. And on top of that the company had to deal with the issue of bad publicity. But there was no need to worry. Carnival Cruise Lines was still able to make millions of dollars for its shareholders.

Wednesday, 20th of March 2002
Grand Cayman Islands

Wool over my Eyes
The life raft provided a small spot of shade while I was sitting on the Lido Deck aft. The ship was anchored off the coast of the Grand Cayman Islands and most guests and crewmembers had gone ashore. That left the ship deserted and empty but also with a peaceful atmosphere. Those hours were a good moment to get a bit of reading done. I had the BMJ (British Medical Journal) in my hands but couldn't really concentrate on the article I was trying to read.

My thoughts went back to the early hours of the night before. I had been called around 3:30 am to attend to a crewmember who was found semi-conscious in the corridor. The patient himself gave me only a vague story of what had happened but a fellow crewmember claimed to have witnessed the event leading to his fall into unconsciousness. He gave an account of the symptoms which may have been due to a seizure. The story wasn't entirely convincing and on examination I couldn't find anything wrong with the patient. But I had to take the information given to me at face value and the crewmember was transferred to a hospital once we had arrived the Cayman Islands. Later that morning I heard from a reliable source that the whole incident had been staged. The crewmember had a lot of problems and just needed a break. I knew that some of the workers onboard had tried to pull the wool over my eyes. The classic attempt at getting some time off was to fake the complaint of having diarrhea. This medical condition demands that the crewmember has to be off duty for at least 48 hours according to the company's policy. However, I had learned how to tighten the screw on malingerers. If I had the suspicion that a complaint was not genuine, I demanded a stool sample. It was amazing to see how some of the patients improved within hours. Sickness amongst the workforce onboard a ship cannot be taken lightly. If I sign a crewmember off sick, their colleagues have to do their work. It is not possible to call in a replacement in the middle of a cruise.

Grand Cayman Islands,
seen from the bridge of the ship

Talking to an invisible Group
While I was going through my recollections the sun had changed its position and began to shine straight into my face. With an adjustment of my deckchair, I regained the shade but I still couldn't concentrate on my reading of the medical journal. Instead, I thought about my very first telephone conference which had taken place just the day before. Actually, it had been a bit nerve wrecking. I had received the instructions for it by e-mail and had been told to dial a specific number at the appointed time. At first, I heard nothing, then some crackling noise and finally the babbling of voices – I was in. The physicians of every ship of the Carnival fleet participated. Steve, the head of the medical department at the headquarters in Miami, chaired this virtual meeting.

First, he checked that everybody who should take part was actually "in". The agenda was driven by medical related events which had taken place on Carnival ships. One ship had an outbreak of Norovirus. The symptoms of this illness are quite unpleasant, giving a patient stomach pains, nausea and vomiting as well as a watery diarrhea. After a few days, most people make a full recovery and it is very rarely fatal. Nevertheless, an outbreak on a cruise ship causes major disruptions. The disease spreads through a ship like wildfire, because people live together in close proximity. Very often a whole voyage must be canceled. And, of course, an outbreak of an infectious disease on a cruise ship is not good for PR.

Also, a case of mine was discussed and I was asked to report the case. The attentive reader may remember the event. It was the one where the patient went onto a cruise against the advice of his own doctor. The incident had happened during my first cruise working solo as a ship's physician. The consensus of my colleagues was that the patient shouldn't have been allowed to sail and that it was wrong for the hotel director to have overridden the medical decision. He was probably afraid of bad PR, but he put the patient at risk and took the unnecessary chance of a medical evacuation or diversion of the ship. The conference ended with an announcement from the HQ. Steve heralded that work on a fleet-wide medical computer system had begun and he was hopeful that it could be implemented in a year or so. Well, that would be a miracle. In my experience most IT projects ended being over-budget and delayed. Anyway, finally this strange way of communicating with a group of people without seeing their faces came to an end.

Verandah Deck, starboard side

Life is a Mixed Bag

The dial-in happened just the day before we arrived at the Grand Cayman Islands. At Cayman I always had a quiet afternoon onboard until the passengers were tendered back from the island. I struggled to get comfortable in the deckchair and to focus on my medical journal. I attempted to find out what was happening in the medical world back in the UK. At times I felt professionally isolated. There was only one doctor onboard – little old me. I had nobody to discuss cases with, nobody to talk to who really understood me (professionally). Yes, there were the nurses as part of the medical team. But they didn't understand the pressure of being a doctor. I had the ultimate responsibility for the wellbeing of all souls onboard. The three nurses on this ship shared the shifts between them. As the doctor I was on call 24 hours a day, seven days a week for six months. Only when the ship was in port I got a break for a few hours. And within the medical team was still a "them" (the nurses) and "me" (the doctor) feeling. We all were health providers, but I was not part of their nursing team. On the other hand, as a head of department and senior officer I had quite a few privileges which they had not. And, of course, I enjoyed a higher salary. Hence the position of a ship's physician was a mixed bag with some favorable and some negative aspects. Like so many other things in life.

Saturday, 23rd of March 2002
Tampa, Florida, USA

I-95 – not an Interstate Road

That day was "Immigration Day". All crewmembers needed to have their passports inspected by US immigration officers. At 7 am I made my way to the back of the Promenade Deck. It was a beautiful morning. The air was still cool, and the sun sent its first beams across the carbor of Tampa. Crewmembers were waiting in a very long line outside the aft (rear) lounge. But everything was well organized. At the entrance were the pursers to hand out the passports. With my passport in hand, I joined the queue waiting to be processed. I didn't "pull rank" as a few of my fellow senior officers did, bypassing the waiting crowd to get ahead of the line. I thought that is not the way to behave. A senior officer should set an example and be disciplined like all the others. After a ten-minute wait or so, it was my turn. I stepped forward to the desk to speak with one of the immigration officers and answer his questions: What is your position onboard? When does your contract end? He looked at my passport and made an entry in a long list. Then my "I-95" (a US immigration card) got a new expiry date. This piece of paper (which had the size of a small post card) together with my ship's ID, allowed me to go ashore at any US port. The passport was handed back to a purser at the end of the process. Since 9/11 the immigration rules had become tighter and tighter. Even for crewmembers who suffer a medical emergency, lengthy paperwork was required in order to get them into the US for treatment at a hospital.

Tampa seen from the Lido Deck

With the renewed I-95 in my pocket I proceeded to the Lido Deck where breakfast was served. Having breakfast there and not in the officer's mess was a little routine of mine to celebrate the fact that it was "home port day" – my day off. Eating in the passenger zone was fine as I was not wearing my uniform but civilian clothing. It made me immune against "harassments" by any of the guests.

Art is an Anti-Depressant

After the breakfast I had a little snooze in my cabin. Then I had to make a big decision: what should I do now? The ship was going to be docked in Tampa for another five hours – which meant five hours of freedom for me. I decided to leave the ship for a stroll in the city. I walked along the Hillsborough River in the stinking heat of an early afternoon. As I passed the Tampa Museum of Art, I had an epiphany. The museum was surely air-conditioned and would make a good place to cool down. Besides, a visit there would probably lift my spirits – so I thought.

I felt a bit low that day without knowing why. Was it just tiredness or was it the heat? However, looking at art always worked like an antidepressant for me. My visit to the Tampa Museum of Art began with a walk through a section that displayed artifacts of the Roman Empire – a culture long gone. I wondered: how long will the current cultures last? I then stumbled onto an installation called "River Myths". It consisted of a confusing system of mirrors and it was impossible to avoid looking at my own image. What I saw in the myriad of mirrors was a man in his mid-forties. It forced me to make a quick evaluation. What had I achieved? And what had I not? I realized that what life has to offer gets smaller with each passing year. Dreams in the sense of achievements have always been the essence of my life. Actually, gaining the job of a ship's doctor was a dream come true. Of course, it was quite different from what I had imagined but that is expected. Well, that dream was over as it had become reality – and I had to find another one.

The museum had a wonderful winter garden (with efficient air-conditioning). Upon entering I was welcomed to a celebration of forms and colors. On display were vases of all shapes in a wide range of designs. Their size varied from huge floor vases to ones with the size of an ink pot. I loved the one with a slim shape in subtle green. It was big enough to put an umbrella in it. I imagined…if I bought this piece of art, where would I put it? During my time as a ship's doctor, I didn't have a home as such. All my belongings were in storage at my sister's house. But I didn't mind – because I was free as a bird.

"American Art in the Age of Anxiety" was the title of an exhibition in another part of the museum. It consisted mainly of abstract paintings, a few sculptures and some photographs. For some reason I liked this exhibition. It left a lot of room for interpretation and stimulated my imagination. What is art anyway? Maybe the sentence "L'art pour l'art" (art for art's sake) is to the point.

Hillsborough River, Tampa, Florida

Tuesday, 26th of March 2002
Cozumel, Mexico

Turning into an able-bodied Seaman
Another Cozumel day. I had a few hours off and was able to visit the Crewmembers Club. The name sounds more posh than the premises actually were. It was basically just a bar on a beach strip but with added facilities that were particularly useful to crewmembers. In addition to food and drink, it offered cheap phone lines, internet access – and girls (if one needed one). For me this place was a refuge. It enabled me to get away from the ship's environment, so I could relax and reflect on past events.

The "Competent Crew Course" came to mind, which had taken place just the day before. Let's see…what is a "bailer"? (a plastic container to scoop water out of small boat) …a "thwart"? (benches in a lifeboat) …a "painter"? (a rope attached to a life raft). And I learnt about other things which were alien to me – the acquired knowledge that was necessary to become an "able-bodied seaman". All crewmembers had to demonstrate that they could get a lifeboat safely into the water and that they were able to inflate a life raft correctly. Instruction classes were held every morning for two weeks. They started at 9:30 am and lasted for about an hour. On occasion I was late for these classes as I was held up by sick patients but I always attend once I had finished my morning surgery. The first officer was in charge of the training, holding lectures in a monotone voice in "Italian English". It was difficult to hear him and even harder to understand what he was talking about. All course participants received a handbook as a reference – a rough guide with poor illustrations. I wondered how we all would fare at the examination at the end of the course. (NB: At the end everybody passed somehow – with or without a little help from the instructor).

Tiredness is Part of the Parcel

The deckchairs at the Crewmembers Club were really comfortable. I stretched myself out to the max and took a few sips from my piña colada. I felt sleepy in the warm sun. Tiredness had become a habit. There were all sorts of reasons for being worn-out. But the main cause was the numerous medical emergencies I had to deal with. Just the night before coming to Cozumel I had been called to see a guest. I attend to him for abdominal pain at 2 am in the morning. It turned out to be a GI (gastro-intestinal) bleed, meaning this gentleman was bleeding from his guts. As a result, I had another restless night and yet another "performance" on the pier the next morning. After the ambulance had left with flashing lights and a howling siren, I had to return to the infirmary to commence my morning surgery. And to make that day a complete fiasco there was a boat drill later that morning. Subsequently, I had to stand on the outer deck with a life vest around my neck and a two-way radio in hand for more than an hour. The tropical sun grilled me nicely to a "well done" German sausage. Thus, lying in the shade under a palm tree with a cold drink in hand was just what the doctor had ordered for himself. Sadly, the reprieve would last only for two hours as I had to go back to the ship for my afternoon surgery. But until then I decided to do nothing but relax.

Waiting for customers, Cozumel

An "Oscar" for Denzel

Cozumel, an island off the coast of Mexico, was part of the repetitive itinerary of the "Jube". Once the ship had docked at the island's pier, I usually took a stroll down the promenade towards the town center. During my stroll I passed a few tourist facilities: diving clubs, boat hires, hotels, restaurants and the like. The town itself was full of clubs and bars – as well as drinking and drunken tourists. Most of them were Americans and quite a few of them under drinking age. In the US no one can have a drink under the age of 21. It is possible to join the US Army at the age of 18 and to kill someone legally (or get killed) but having an alcoholic drink at that age was still illegal. Anyway, far more dangerous things were (and are) consumed by teenagers than alcohol.

After a meal and a bit of shopping in the town, I had to go back to the ship for my afternoon surgery. But for the evening I was scheduled to be off duty as the ship wasn't going to leave Cozumel until 10 pm. I wasn't so sure what I was going do with the evening. Maybe I should go for a drink at the Crazy Pelican, my favorite bar near the pier. Or just watch television in my cabin. Incidentally, I had watched the Oscars Ceremony the other day. What a show! Denzel Washington got the prize of best actor. He was a dignified winner, unlike the best actress. She cried throughout her reception speech. I cannot remember her name, but she was rather pathetic.

The highlight of the whole show for me was the appearance of Robert Redford. He got an honorary award. In his acceptance speech he pointed out what is wrong with the American film industry: it's all about the money. He supported independent filmmakers. I think he was right. In the US, movies are seen as a product which has to generate a profit. In Europe movies are more seen as a form of art.

The Promenade, Cozumel, Mexico

Ah, I forgot to mention that I had a haircut a few days earlier. The *Jubilee* has its own hair salon onboard and guess what? Peter, the hairdresser who served me, was from Penryn, a little village in Cornwall. I had lived in Cornwall for a while. What a small world! While Peter cut my hair, he told me that he had married a girl from Thailand. They had met on another ship on which both of them were working. It was one of those "ship's marriages" with partners who have very different cultural backgrounds. Would the marriage survive after the couple quit ship's life and moved on to an onshore existence? They would find out…but there are often questions for some of them (mainly the men) who have married someone from a developing country. They may have to ask themselves whether their partner has married them or their passport.

Easter Sunday, 31ˢᵗ of March 2002
Onboard the M/S Jubilee, Caribbean Sea

A Thrill, not a Drill
The day began with my usual Kellogg's All Bran cereal for breakfast in the officer's mess. Little did I know that it was the start of a particularly unusual day – that of my first 'MedEvac' (medical evacuation).

There was nothing exciting about my morning surgery. I was treating the usual coughs, sore throats and muscle aches. But then I received a call that someone had fallen gravely ill. A young woman, a waitress, had a very sore tummy and felt nauseated. She was brought to the infirmary, and after a thorough assessment, I made the diagnosis of an acute appendicitis. In the movies the ship's doctor operates heroically onboard the swaying ship to safe the woman's life. She of course falls in love with the doctor – or something along those lines.

But I was starring in another film. Half an hour later, I was sitting in the captain's office discussing with him the situation. Fred, the hotel director, was also present, partly because he needed to communicate the changes to the cruise to the guests, but also because he was the supervisor of the patient. We discussed the options open to us: A diversion of the ship to the nearest port? Speeding up the ship to arrive at our destination earlier? Or should we go for a helicopter evacuation? My task was to talk to the US Coast Guard. Fortunately, I was able to persuade the Flight Surgeon to organize an evacuation. But the situation was complicated. The Coast Guard was very busy and the only helicopter available was in the east of Florida and had to refuel. Subsequently, the ship had to divert towards Key West in order to shorten the time towards a rendezvous. The ETA (estimated time of arrival) of the helicopter was expected to be at 1600 hours (4 pm). It was 2:30 pm when I left the captain's office to make my way to the infirmary. There was no time to waste. I had to get the patient ready for the "evac" (evacuation). My first task was to explain to an anxious young woman what was going to happen. That was somewhat of a challenge, as she was from Croatia and her English language skills were rather limited. So, I recruited a fellow countryman of hers who translated my instructions: Don't be afraid, keep your eyes closed and your arms under the blanket. One of the nurses will be coming with you all the way.

USCG helicopter

Preparations

Nurse Sonia was the lucky one who was assigned to accompany the patient for the helicopter ride to the hospital. The final hour before the evacuation was quite hectic. Numerous people came to the infirmary for one reason or another. There were lots of papers which required my signature, not only the medical report, but also immigration papers, security clearance and so on. I also had to make many phone calls to keep the relevant department heads informed and to ensure and coordinate their support for the impending evacuation.

Finally, I received the message: 30 minutes until rendezvous. It was time to get the patient ready for the transfer. The frightened woman was given a lifejacket and wrapped up in a warm blanket before she was laid into a basket stretcher. All tubes were secured, and the needed medical equipment was set up for transport. It took six guys to carry the patient and the medical gear. Three security officers led the little procession. They had the difficult job of clearing the way – there were plenty of interested onlookers who needed to be pushed aside. I was walking directly behind the stretcher, keeping an eye on the patient. Behind me were my three nurses. It was impossible to use the elevator as the stretcher wouldn't fit in there. For that reason we had to walk up the stairs deck by deck while the ship's loudspeakers made an announcement: "Dear guests, a fellow passenger (which was not true, but made the crowd probably more sympathetic) is in need of urgent medical care. An emergency disembarkation will take place in a few moments. For this reason, parts of the Lido Deck are not accessible. Thank you for your understanding!"

At last, we arrived on the Upper Deck aft, at the very back of the ship. We were greeted by a huge gallery of spectators behind the security line and on all upper decks. The ship's speed was kept constant and the course steady. The weather was fine with bright sunshine and only a light breeze. The stage was set and the audience attentive – the "performance" could begin.

Hovering over the ship

Let the Show begin
The helicopter approached the ship from the port (left) side. It hovered over the deck for a quite a while before a rescue basket was lowered on a wire. The device looked like a metal shopping cart without the wheels and in it sat the corpsman (paramedic). Once the basket hit the deck the corpsman climbed out of the basket and walked towards me. With a broad smile he asked: "How is it going, doc?" and shook my hand. He was a good-looking fellow with broad shoulders and a strong grip. I gave him a quick rundown of the medical situation. This guy knew what he was doing; he asked all the right questions. Then he went into swift but deceive action. Over the radio he told the pilot the order of the evacuation: first the nurse, then the patient, and at last himself.

The winchman in action

The nurse, Sonia, climbed into the rescue basket to start her journey up into the helicopter. A rope attached to the basket was held by the corpsman to stabilize it during the ascent but it was of no avail. The basket swayed and turned during the winch up. Sonia told me later that the trip had felt like a roller coaster ride. Finally, the winchman got hold of the basket and dragged it into the helicopter.

Once the nurse was safely onboard the helicopter a stretcher was lowered onto the deck. It was light but sturdy, made of a strong wire mesh. The corpsman detached it from the wire and the helicopter veered off but kept following the ship. John, the lead nurse, the corpsman, and I transferred the anxious patient into the special stretcher. We then carried the stretcher to the pick-up area of the deck. On a radio signal from the corpsman the helicopter came closer again until it hovered right above our heads. The engine noise was unbelievable. I then understood why we had been equipped with ear plugs. The wire came down again and was attached to the holding system of the stretcher. A hand signal given by the corpsman initiated the winch up. The stretcher went up into the air. This time the ride up to the helicopter was fairly smooth. There was only a little swaying and the winchman had no trouble pulling the stretcher into the cabin of the aircraft.

The corpsman being winched up

Finally, it was the turn of the corpsman to get up. John and I received a goodbye and a handshake from him and he then attached the wire onto his harness. With an ease and coolness that would have made even James Bond envious, he was pulled up to the helicopter and then swung himself into the hatch. The helicopter then veered off to make its journey to the hospital in Key West at the tip of Florida.

Once the aircraft was gone it was curtains for the "evac show". The spectators stashed their cameras away and the crowds dispersed. The two remaining nurses and I made our way back to the infirmary where the duties of the daily routine were waiting for us.

Up, up, and away

A Boat called *Kaylee Ray*

At 11 am sharp, I was standing at the quayside in Cozumel on the lookout for my crew. It was not the medical crew I was looking for, but a few hands needed to man a sailing boat. That day I had managed to finish my morning surgery bang on time and the plan was to go for a sailing trip. I had hired a boat for the day and invited the usual suspects. Some of my fellow workers, people I normally hang out with, were destined to join me. Those included were the nurses, Sonia and John, as well as Mandy and Robert, a couple who worked on the cruise ship as musicians. In addition, a lady called Lydia was supposed to join us. She was a guest on the current cruise, visiting her sister, Sonia, the nurse. *So, where are they all?* I asked myself standing in the heat of the Mexican sun.

After waiting for a while longer, I decided to make my way to the pick-up point for the boat. It was just a few hundred yards down the promenade, near the Hotel Casa del Mar. Maybe my "crew" would be there - and bingo! There they were, guarding the provisions – a huge plastic tub filled with ice and cold drinks, as well as a gigantic package of sandwiches. However, the charter agent didn't appear at the agreed time of 11:30 am. A phone call to the agent exposed our ignorance. We had simply got the time wrong. Well, not really. We were on ships' time, which was one hour ahead of the local time in Cozumel. I had never realized that discrepancy during my many visits to the island until then. Eventually, a white inflatable Zodiac boat appeared to get us to the sailing boat.

The Kaylee Ray

It was a wild ride. The boat hopped over the waves while the wind blew sea spray into our faces. We sped along the coastline, passing a few cruise ships on the way. After a 15-minute journey, the Zodiac got alongside the *Kaylee Ray*, a 27-foot sailing boat. We jumped onboard, stowed our provisions and after a short introduction to the boat by the charter agent we were able to set sail. I was the only one who had a sailing license. Still, I was glad that I had taken a refresher lesson on how to handle a larger boat just a week earlier during a home port day in Tampa.

Relationships – a Debate

And so the fun began. We enjoyed the food and drink whilst sailing along the coast of Cozumel. The boat moved smoothly through the deep blue water and I was able to keep a steady course northward, even with a can of beer in one hand. This was the time to relax – and to gossip. Gossiping was one, well *the*, biggest activity among crewmembers. We talked about the special concept of an affiliation between a man and a woman: that of a ships' relationship. This kind

52

of bond involving crewmembers has a limited shelf-life. It may last a day, a week or a month. The longest would be the period of the contracted time. Once the assignment of a crewmember comes to an end, so does the relationship. Some couples, who wanted to stay together, asked for a contract to be assigned to the same vessel. Although that was a very rare occurrence because it was incredibly difficult to organize. Even married couples had problems getting contracts for the same ship.

An interesting discussion evolved concerning the morality of ships' relationships. Some argued that having a relationship onboard, while married, cannot be construed as cheating. Many of us knew about couples among the crew who had married partners onshore back home. Personally, I was pretty sure that the wives of sea officers know that it is impossible to tie a knot into a "willie" (penis) for months on end. And it appeared that these wives (or husbands) accepted short-term relationships onboard a ship – as long as it was done discreetly and their partner continued to be a husband (or wife) and a parent for their kids. But this kind of arrangement can lead to awkward situations when the beloved wife or husband comes onboard for visits to the ship. I remember a captain's dinner attended by the wife of one of the senior officers. The waitress who served the food was the very person this officer was having an affair with at the time – and everybody knew it! Maybe even his wife too. That evening I found the atmosphere during the dinner very unsettling, and I made my excuses to escape as soon as possible.

Relationships among crewmembers were widespread for obvious reasons. An assignment for six or even nine months is a long, long time. As a result, casual affairs were a common occurrence, with all the consequences attached to them. Undesired events happened despite the fact that condoms were available 24/7, free of charge, discreetly displayed in a box near the infirmary. Nevertheless, I frequently had to treat cases of STDs (sexually transmitted diseases) among crewmembers. Even more tricky to handle were unwanted pregnancies. The company paid for medical care but not for abortions. Still, I helped the women to make the necessary arrangements for a procedure in a reputable hospital - if that was what they wanted. But had to be paid for by her or her partner.

"The gang"
(From left: Ship's doctor,
lead nurse John, nurse Sonia)

About "Coning"
As we sailed in the warm waters of the Caribbean Sea another hot topic was debated: that of "coning". The term referred to guests, as "cones". Why, one might ask? Well, there is a movie called *Coneheads* which is about aliens from outer space with heads shaped like cones. I had never watched that movie, but apparently these individuals eat and drink a lot. And that is what the guests do on a cruise ship – hence the nickname for them. Now, "coning" meant that a

crewmember had a (mainly short-term) relationship with a guest. "Going coning" was an expression for trawling in the ship's disco or other suitable places to pick up a guest. Coning was officially not allowed, of course, but quietly tolerated as long as it was done discreetly. A few senior officers were heavily into coning. Allegedly, the chief engineer spent more time in the ship's bars then in the engine room. And it was rumoured that he was quite successful in coning. It must have been his uniform which contributed to his success. He himself was not Robert Redford material.

Time flew by as we discussed the different aspects of relationships during our sailing trip that afternoon. John's face became increasingly red. Was it the sun or the beer that was to blame? Or both? After two hours of sailing, we had reached the north end of Cozumel. I tried to steer the boat into a secluded bay but, alas, the water was too shallow for that and I had to make a full turn. It was time to return to the ship anyway, my afternoon surgery was due to start fairly soon. Once back on shore we realized that we had overestimated our requirement for drinks. There were still plenty of beer bottles and soda cans left which filled several cooling boxes. We decided to bring them back onboard the ship for later consumption. Of course, the security guys at the gangway wanted to know what was in the containers. "The catch of the day," we answered. But they didn't believe us and we had to put the boxes through the scanner.

Thursday, 11th of April 2002.
Ybor City, Tampa, Florida, USA

The Penguin Parade

I was off duty as it was a home port day. That day I felt a bit tired. Why? Well, I had attended a party the night before. For a few hours I had joined a few crewmember friends on the Panorama Deck to share music, wine and lively conversations with them. The occasion was the celebration of Lydia's birthday. She had joined the ship for two cruises. As she was the sister of my nurse Sonia, her voyage was low-cost. She got the eight days onboard, which included food and all entertainment, for only US $45 (the port fee). The only snag was that she had to stay in the berth of her sister Sonia, who had only an indoor cabin near the workshops. It was basically a dark, smelly hole with two bunk beds.

And there was more to celebrate than a birthday: the arrival of the new formal uniform for my appearance at the "Penguin Parade". This event was held on the second evening of every cruise. Why that nickname? Well, all senior officers (including the ship's doctor) had to wear their formal attire that evening. And with the black trousers and white dinner jacket we all looked like penguins (see photo). Plus, we paraded on stage to be introduced to the guests, hence the name of this event.

In the beginning it was quite fun to appear in front of hundreds of people to be introduced as the doctor onboard the ship. After a while the event became a bit stale and repetitive. I also realized that my appearance actually advertised the services of the infirmary and merely created additional work for me. Quite a few guests came to see me to sort out their chronic back pain or other ongoing health problems because they had learnt that the ship has a doctor onboard.

After the Penguin Parade a dinner was held for all senior personnel at the captain's table. That was a rather stiff event and we often ended up discussing work related issues. And the food was not great either. But the parade and the captain's dinner were part of my duties. That was until I found out that the ship's doctor was not obliged to participate if he has deal with a medical emergency. And as it happened I had quite a few of those during various penguin parades (wink, wink!).

In formal uniform

Cigars and History

Well, what about my home port day? I always felt that I had to do something on those days, and not just sleeping or hanging out in a café. So, that day I decided to visit Ybor City, a district in the northeast of Tampa. This part of town is famous for its well-preserved old houses from the golden times of cigar making. Along its main road, the 7th Avenue, I passed a house built in Spanish-Cuban style of the late nineteenth century. It still had balconies with wrought-iron banisters. I wandered down the streets of Ybor City quite early in the day. Many shops were still closed and only a few people were about. The temperature was quite pleasant that day, warm but with crisp air.

Former social club, Ybor City, Tampa

Further down the avenue was a visitors' center with a little museum. It explained why that part of Tampa is called Ybor City. In 1885 Vincente Martinez Ybor had come to Florida to manufacture cigars. He was born in Spain but lived in Cuba where he produced cigars. In 1869 he moved his production to Key West, owing to political unrest on the island of Cuba. But Key West wasn't suitable either. The space available there to expand production was very limited and he had problems with the labor force. Subsequently, he took the opportunity to move production again when 40 acres of land were offered to him near Tampa in 1885. But the terrain had to be developed. When Ybor arrived there in 1886 the land was bare apart from alligators and stray dogs living on it. He had to establish the whole infrastructure, including basic features such as water supply and electricity. To attract skilled workers, he created decent housing for them around his factory and in a way he shaped his own city – Ybor City.

Ybor City Cigar Factory (Wikipedia)

People from all over the world came to help to produce cigars. Most of them came from Cuba or Spain. But a significant number of Italians also immigrated to work for Ybor as he offered good working conditions. The salary depended on the output. On average a worker could roll 125 cigars per day. That would give him an income of US $ 80 per week (an engineer earned around US $ 30 p/w at the time). There were also free cigars for the workers, although I suspect they had to roll their own. Each employee could take breaks as it pleased him (only men were employed). Hundreds of workers would sit at long tables to produce the cigars. In the middle of the hall was a little podium – for the lecturer. He would sit there on a chair to read to the workforce, mainly novels and newspaper articles – but also poetry. The lecturer was paid by the workers (25 cents per worker, per week). But the employer didn't like this arrangement. He was suspicious of the reading material, believing it could be something subversive. So he banned the lecturer. The consequence was a strike – with the result that the lecturer was replaced by a radio.

W.T. Grant Co. building, Ybor City

Nevertheless, Ybor City thrived. Other cigar manufacturers came and at the time Tampa had the largest cigar production in the world. The workers were well off and enjoyed a rich cultural life through social clubs – run and financed by them. The good life in Ybor city ended abruptly with the great depression in the 1930s. Mechanization and the increasing popularity of cigarettes added to the decline. By the late 1960s Ybor City was virtually abandoned. But in 1990s the area recovered as shops, cafes, bars and nightclubs moved into the district and quite a few buildings were restored.

Enjoying a beer in Ybor City

No Groundhog Day for me!
After spending almost two hours at the visitors' center, I was thirsty and hungry. And in any case, it was lunch time. The area was not short of promising eating places. I settled for a restaurant which offered a good view from its balcony. From there I could see the tracks of a streetcar line, which was under reconstruction and due to be opened in October that year. As I munched my lunch and slurped the freshly drafted beer, I contemplated whether I would be around for the opening of the tram line. In fact, I had no clue at the time where I would be in October. Always on the move – that's what I was. But I had (and have) no regrets. The world is such a big place and there is so much to see. I imagined how it would be making a living as a doctor in England. I would drive to work after a quick breakfast and then face an endless stream of patients for a whole day. The only interruption might be to sit in a car to drive to sick patients at their home. Lunch would be a sandwich at the steering wheel. In the evening I might have just the power to watch the news after dinner, before going to bed, dead tired. I have been there: life like in the movie *Groundhog Day* – one day exactly the same as the other. Such kind of existence is not for me. That day in Ybor City I was glad not to know where I would be in a few months' time.

Friday, 12 of April 2002
Key West, Florida

A Man on a Mission
I was lucky enough to finish my morning surgery on time. The ship had docked at the downtown harbor of Key West. With a bounce in my steps, I walked across the gangway to get onshore. My destination was the shopping area of the town. That day I was a man on a mission:

to buy a gift for John, the lead nurse. His time was up, and he was on his last cruise. In two days, he would fly back home to the UK.

Duval Street, Key West

It was a sunny day, but the temperature was bearable as it was still springtime. As I walked down Duval Street, I joined loads of tourists. Along the street were plenty of bars, restaurants and (more importantly for me that day) shops. I considered my options. Would it be a t-shirt? And, if so, plain or with a print? With an ornament or a picture? Or with a joke written on it? Wanna hear an example? Here goes: "I gave up smoking, drinking and sex. It was the most terrifying five minutes of my life." Hm…maybe something else. There were plenty of jewelry stores along Duval Street, but I gave that a miss – too personal. And it could be misconstrued. John was gay after all. Maybe I should get him a box of cigars. I found tobacco shops on almost every corner. But the stuff didn't come from Cuba because of the embargo – so no good. At the end I settled for a Zippo lighter as John (like so many nurses) was a smoker. Still, I wasn't sure whether that gift was ethical. I shouldn't encourage smoking as a doctor.

After my short shopping spree, it was time for lunch. I felt I had earned it – shopping is such an exhausting occupation. I found a nice restaurant with seating in a garden. A table under the shade of a huge tree was the right place for me. I ordered a large beer. A Foster's lager imported from Australia. Not the local stuff. American beer is, to my German taste buds, just colored water. I have never understood how Americans managed to create a light version from that already thin liquor.

It was around midday and too hot to eat anything substantial so I had (for a change) some healthy stuff: just a salad. Then I turned my attention to *USA Today*, a newspaper I had bought earlier. First things first: the sport section. The major golf tournament of the year was on: The Masters in Atlanta, Georgia. It looked good for Tiger Woods. He may win this thing again to get his third Green Jacket. (My apologies to all non-Golfers: you may not understand what I am talking about).

89 Steps to a Green View

After lunch I still had two hours until I had to be back on the ship. What to do with this extra time? I decided to climb the lighthouse of Key West. According to the information board at the entrance it had been erected in 1848. At the top, 15 meters above the ground, it was equipped with 13 lamps surrounded by reflectors. In 1894 another six meters of height were added to surmount the taller buildings of Key West. The home of Ernest Hemmingway was actually close by and legend has it that he bought the house because of its proximity to the lighthouse.

The light from the tower could guide him home after a night of heavy drinking at Sloppy Joe's Bar. The story is probably not true but says something about Hemmingway's reputation.

The lighthouse was decommissioned in 1969 and together with the living quarters of the keeper converted into a museum in 1972. A small exhibition in the museum explained the necessity of the lighthouse. There are countless reefs around the Florida Keys and many ships became victim to them. A few impressive photos of damaged and sunk ships were on display. The daily life of the lighthouse guard was also explained. It appeared to be a quite tedious job, walking up and down the many stairs of the tower to maintain the light.

Light House, Key West

As a matter of fact, I had to take 89 steps to get to the top of the lighthouse - I counted them on my way up. Yet, the climb was worth the effort. I was rewarded with a magnificent view and I discovered that Key West looks actually quite green from above. In the distance I could see the harbor with the cruise ships. "My" ship the *M/S Jubilee* was clearly identifiable with its red and blue funnel. Seeing the ship reminded me that I had to hurry back. Duty called. My afternoon surgery was due to start in half an hour.

View over Key West

The sudden end of a Party

The whole medical team (the three nurses and me) had a little get-together in the infirmary yesterday evening. We had planned to have tea and cake to mark the last day of John's contract. He was scheduled to leave the ship in Tampa the following day. He was desperate to get home to the UK after four months of duty. We had just sat down to dive into a cream cake when my pager went off. I was informed that a guest had severe difficulties breathing. It turned out that she had a "bad lung". The medical term for her illness was COAD (chronic obstructive airways disease). It took a lot of medication and TLC (tender loving care) to stabilize the patient. The medication came from my side and the TLC from the nurses. We were just about to go for a late dinner, when a second emergency cropped up. Again, it was a guest with problems to breath. She had the same problem but for a different reason. This lady had water in her lungs (pulmonary oedema). It seemed that similar problems come in batches.

Well, that was definitely the end of the planned goodbye party. By around midnight the immediate crisis was under control. But we had two very sick patients in our little infirmary. The task was to get them through the night until the ship arrived in Tampa the next morning. The nurses took turns to look after the patients and would call me when needed. I ensured that John got a break to go to his cabin get his packing done. That was around 2 am. Poor John didn't have the opportunity to say goodbye to any of his friends onboard.

Looking for the right medication

Around 7 am I reviewed the patients together with an exhausted John. The good news was that the two ladies were in a stable condition. An hour later the ship arrived in Tampa. Two ambulances with flashing blue lights were waiting at the quay to transport our patients to the hospital. It felt a bit crowded when the ambulance crews came onboard to retrieve them. Four paramedics with two stretchers and all their equipment was a bit too much for our tiny infirmary. After a thorough hand-over to the ambulance crews, the patients were wheeled out of the infirmary. It was quite a crowd that moved towards the ship's exit. The group consisted of the two patients on a stretcher, the four paramedics, relatives of the patients, three security guys, the chief purser and finally John and me. It was a miracle how we managed to squeeze through the maze of corridors and hatches. But finally, we arrived at the gangway. John and I watched the ambulances as they left the quay in the glow of the rising morning sun. John had finished his contract with a big bang. I shook his hand, to thank him for all his help and wished him well for his new life in the UK. He had just half an hour to clear his cabin and to leave the ship.

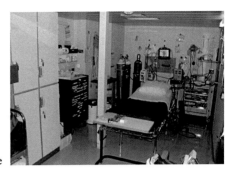

***Crash room, infirmary, M/S* Jubilee**

Tour de Tourist

It was a long day, but a great one. For the first time I had the chance to see the ruins of a Mayan settlement. Why? Because the *Jubilee* had arrived early in Cozumel to spend a few additional hours in port. The spare time was needed to replace a few vital parts in the engine room. Due to the early arrival the whole tour schedule was changed to the morning. That enabled me to join the excursion to Tulum and to be back in time for my afternoon surgery.

Pier at Playa del Carmen, Mexico

Shree, a girl from the paymaster's office, had helped me to get onto this tour. Shore excursions for senior officers such as I were free of charge. That was one of the perks working as a doctor on a cruise ship. At 10 am Shree and I joined a group of about 12 guests in one of the lounges of the ship, waiting to set off. The first leg of the journey was a boat ride from the island of Cozumel to the resort of Playa del Carmen on the mainland. It was a quick ride of just 15 minutes but it was a bumpy crossing as the boat carrying us was small and quite old. It struggled to cope with the swell of the Caribbean Sea. Still, it felt good to escape the ship and to leave everything behind.

The waterfront of Playa del Carmen consisted mainly of hotels, bars, cafés and shops. We didn't see the place as such as we were herded from the pier straight onto a coach. We boarded the bus to join other tourists, mainly from the US. They were staying in various local hotels and had booked the same tour. From then on, Shree and I were part of a 40 person-strong tourist group. After just few minutes we left Playa del Carmen and rolled southwards along the coast following the Mexican Highway 307.

Onboard the bus was a Mexican tour guide who talked to the crowd in perfect English, but with a strong Spanish accent. After cracking a few jokes about "Mexican meets gringo", he provided some information about the Mayas. They were more a culture than an ethnic group. The area of Mayan settlements covered large parts of Central America, including Mexico. The height of the Mayan civilisation was between 250 and 900 AD. There was no empire, but a collection of independent kingdoms which shared culture, language and religious rituals. The Mayan architecture was quite advanced, and they built some impressive cities. They also had advanced mathematical and astronomical knowledge and developed a sophisticated trading system. But that didn't keep them from making human sacrifices to their gods.

After this short deviation into the past the guide returned to issues of the imminent present and announced a refreshment stop. Yeah right! It was nothing of that sort, but a tourist trap. A little shop next to the highway sold the usual crap: t-shirts, cheap jewellery and souvenirs "Made in China". And, yes, it was possible to buy a cold soft drink or some ice cream. Shree and I were having none of it and sat just under a parasol and exchanged ship's gossip for half an hour.

In front of El Castillo, Tulum

Heat and knowledge Overload
Finally, we arrived at Tulum. Stepping out of the air-conditioned coach into the midday heat was quite a shock to the system. And, of course, our group was not the only one visiting the Mayan site that day. The place was crawling with gringos. An official tour guide rounded us up to take us from the huge car park to the actual site. The walk was quite pleasant as it led through a cool forest.

The site itself was right at the edge of a cliff. The guide explained that Tulum was known as the city of dawn since the sun rises over the coastline. This ancient city had been built like a fortress, surrounded by high walls except the side facing the Caribbean Sea, where the cliffs provided a natural defence. Not much was left of the ancient city, just the walls. One of the exceptions is El Castillo (the castle), which dominates the site as it stands in the centre of this little community. It contained a shrine and may have once been used as a watch tower.

Shade seekers, Tulum

Our group followed the guide through the rubble of the buildings which had housed about 1,200 people at the time. Since religion dominated the lives of the Mayas these ancient dwellings had several ceremonial centres. The guide then spoke about the amazing astronomical knowledge the Mayas had, how they developed an elaborate calendar and that they were able to predict the movements of the moon. Even the eclipse of the sun had been predicted by them… and that was the last I can remember from the guide's speech. My brain had become a bit mushy from the heat and I had to leave the group to find a shaded place. Shree joined me and we decided to go down to the water to cool down.

The Beach at Tulum

Tequila or Petrol?
After clambering down a staircase alongside the steep cliffs, we reached a beautiful beach. Alas, there was no escape from the crowds. I heard languages from all over the world – including German. It appeared that one can come across my fellow countrymen bloody everywhere!

Shree and I wandered back to the entrance to find something to eat and drink. And bingo! There were not only the usual souvenir stands but a "little America" with McDonalds, KFC and the like. We settled for a sandwich at Subway. Yes, it was American food, but awfully good! (According to my taste). It went down well with a bottle of ice-cold coke. Especially after all the heat and dust we had endured on the journey. Afterwards we felt strong enough to board the coach again to get back.

My recollection of the return journey is actually a bit hazy. Partly because I was incredibly tired from the tour and partly due to the tequila which was distributed throughout the bus. The stuff was pretty lethal – close to petrol, but free. The ferry ride to the ship was rougher than I had remembered on the way out. Then again, the breeze on the boat sobered me up quite a bit and a cold shower on the ship made me entirely fit for my afternoon surgery.

Monday, 29th of April 2002
Tampa, Florida

From Routine to Excitement

Another day, another home port day. I had spent a few hours on a sailing boat, cruising across Tampa Bay, so I was in a cheery mood when I returned to the ship. As I entered the infirmary to start my 5 pm surgery, I could hear the roar of the engine and felt the vibrations of the ship. The *Jubilee* had left the quay and was under way to Cozumel. Before seeing patients, I checked my professional e-mails. Fortunately, I had acquired the skill of sifting through a large number of mails in a short period of time. The number of messages I received every day was mind boggling. Well, it took just a click and the ship's doctor was copied on this or that piece of information. The majority of messages was not relevant for me or my department. Most of the e-mails were boring, some interesting, and a few amusing. One of the more entertaining mails was the purser's report. It stated all the incidents which had happened during the last cruise. For instance, a couple demanded a second cabin (probably on course towards a divorce). The laundry ruined a dress worth US $ 900 (well, who is going to believe that?). The music during a wedding ceremony was played too fast (maybe somebody wanted to speed up the procedure). And then there always a long list of lost or damaged luggage (genuine or not – who knows?)

My first patient that evening was a crewmember. He had a terrible headache, didn't like bright lights, had a temperature and his neck felt a bit stiff. Pulling everything together what did I get as a diagnosis? Jesus! Well, not him, but possibly meningitis, a serious infection of the central nervous

LAW & ORDER
HILLSBOROUGH

Ill Passenger Removed From Carnival Cruise

TAMPA — A Carnival cruise ship heading to Cozumel was ordered back to Tampa on Monday night after a passenger was found to be possibly infected with meningitis.

Coast Guard Cmdr. Scott Ferguson issued a return order to the cruise ship Jubilee about 7:30 p.m., and initially wanted to quarantine the passengers at the Port of Tampa, Coast Guard spokesman Robert Suddarth said.

After consulting with medical personnel on the ship, Ferguson rescinded the order and sent a Coast Guard rescue ship to meet the Jubilee. The ill passenger was transported to Bayfront Medical Center.

The Jubilee, which can carry up to 1,486 passengers and 670 crew members, had not made it past the Sunshine Skyway when the passenger reported feeling ill to medical staff on board. A doctor on the ship determined the passenger might be infected with meningitis, a contagious airborne disease that can result in death.

The ship was allowed to resume its journey to Cozumel.

DUI Charges Filed

system which can cause brain damage or even death. And it is highly contagious. However, even if that was the case, I had to keep calm and behave professionally. The most important task was to isolate the patient in the infirmary. The next thing to do was to speak with the captain on the bridge to discuss the situation. We decided to notify the USCG (United States Coast Guard) to request advice. First, they wanted to know all the maritime stuff like our

64

position, course, speed of the ship, visibility, and all that. Then it was my turn to explain the medical situation. And that was not as easy as having a telephone conversation. I had to talk via a two-way radio. But I learned quickly to say "over" after every sentence and then to wait for the reply. Otherwise, one speaks over the other. Spelling names required me to give each letter a name to make it clear which one was meant. Like Tango for "T" or Bravo for "B", and so on. My knowledge of the "NATO alphabet", I had acquired during my time in the German Army, became handy in that situation. The conversation ended with "stand by" and "over and out", meaning the Coast Guard would think about the situation and then notify us of their decision.

From Excitement to a Thrill
I returned to the infirmary where the patient had been confined to a side room. The nurses wore gowns, gloves, face masks, hoods and protective glasses. And so did I, when I spoke to the patient again. We all must have looked quite scary to him. In any case, he was understandably pretty anxious of what was happening. I tried to calm him down and explained the situation. Still, I needed the names of everyone with whom he had close contact with during the past 24 hours. The patient had already his dose of prophylactic antibiotics but we had to do the contact tracing as well.

Ship's Doctor at his desk
onboard the M/S **Jubilee**

In order to get this done, a great deal of organization and improvisation was required. I got the hotel director involved to track down the crewmembers who may have been infected. Soon a constant stream of people was coming to the infirmary. But we were prepared. At a table near the entrance, we dished out the prophylactic antibiotics. The situation was a little bit chaotic, but exceedingly exciting at the same time – and I was in the middle of it! I admit that I enjoyed the thrill. This kind of work was certainly far more stimulating than the coughs and colds I dealt with in a normal doctor's surgery. Every person who came for the antibiotics was asked about symptoms. One of the stewards was complaining of a headache. He was from Indonesia and spoke only a little English, so I conscripted a fellow countryman to translate. After taking a thorough medical history and conducting a careful examination I determined that he had a simple headache. He was (thank god!) not a second case of meningitis.

In between all these activities, I was informed that the USCG had decided to put the ship under quarantine and that we were ordered to return to Tampa. That meant a whole day of the cruise would be lost. But just half an hour later I got a call from the company's HQ that the situation had changed. The sick crewmember should be disembarked and a USCG boat would pick the patient up and get him to a hospital onshore. Hence, the *Jubilee* would then be able to continue its cruise to Mexico. Hm… I wondered why the original decision had been reversed.

A delay to the cruise would certainly mess up the schedule and would have cost Carnival quite a bit of money. Maybe someone higher up in the company had called someone with authority to get another decision on this difficult situation.

Well, that didn't matter to me. I had to get the show onto the road – or onto the boat to be more precise. The nurses handed out protective gear for everybody involved in the evacuation. That meant the stretcher carriers, the security guys, a few deckhands and of course the medical team had to be dolled-up with gowns, gloves, masks and all that stuff.

A shaky Evacuation

At 6:30 pm I stepped onto a platform on the side of the ship's hull, which was normally used to get the pilot onboard. It was just three by three meters wide and had no railings. The ship couldn't stop for the transfer of the patient because it would drift uncontrollably without any forward motion. Instead, it held a steady course at a constant speed. Night had fallen and it was already pitch dark as I stood on the platform. All I saw were the white heads of breaking waves in the ship's spotlight. After a few minutes I got the call on my handheld radio. The boat from the USCG was approaching the *Jubilee*. And, indeed, I could see some navigation lights coming closer and the boat finally appeared. It was just 10 meters long with a small cabin for the skipper, but it had a large loading area in the back. It was manned by three guys. The boat came alongside, matching the speed of the *Jubilee*. Lines were thrown and the boat was tied to the platform.

Sickbay, Infirmary, M/S Jubilee

My first task was to provide the boat crew with protective equipment. It was more a case of a throwing than a proper hand-over. While I explained the situation to the skipper, things got a bit messy. Suddenly I had the stretcher team with the patient on the platform but the guys on the coastguard boat had not gowned-up and they still had to take their prophylactic antibiotics. Now robust leadership was required. With strong words I ordered the stretcher team back into the ship. Once the guys on the boat were ready, I told the nurse Sonia to come onto the platform. She climbed into the boat to accompany the patient to the hospital. Next, the stretcher with the patient was transferred into the boat. This maneuver was an awfully wobbly affair but ultimately went well. Finally, the ropes were untied, and the coastguard boat disappeared into the dark. That was the end of yet another successful evacuation. Well, not quite. We all had to return to the infirmary, the nurses had to clean up the mess there, and I had to complete plenty of paperwork.

PS: This event made it into the news. A few days later, a fellow crewmember came with the *Tampa Bay Tribune* to the infirmary. The newspaper contained a short article about the incident.

NB: The sick crewmember did well. It turned out that he had just a meningeal irritation (harmless!) and he re-joined the ship a week later.

Thursday, 2ⁿᵈ of May 2002
Cozumel, Mexico

Alarm – Visit from HQ

My morning surgery was somewhat different that day. While I was seeing a bunch of patients, the nurses entertained a visitor. Danielle from the HQ had arrived for a visit while the *Jubilee* was docked in Cozumel. I had met her during my introduction to the company at the beginning of my contract. Danielle was the director of the Crew Medical Department of Carnival Cruise Lines. She was responsible for all health issues concerning crewmembers. It was a hell of a job considering that Carnival had several thousand staff on its ships. Under Danielle's responsibility fell the shore-side health management of the staff. Her department coordinated the medical care of crewmembers in clinics and hospitals in our ports of call. I frequently sent crewmembers to onshore medical facilities for further investigations or treatment. Thus, I had a lot of dealings with her department and herself. She was a bubbly and lively person and I felt sometimes exhausted after a telephone conversation with her. Still, we maintained a good and professional relationship.

Coastline of Cozumel

Having a visitor from the HQ onboard was always stressful. As the head of the medical department, I had to make sure that they were well looked after. For that reason, I ensured that plenty of coffee, juice and nibbles were available upon her arrival. I also stipulated that all three nurses had to be present in the infirmary that morning. They usually leave the ship and head for the beaches once we arrived in Cozumel. Instead, they had a coffee and a chat with Danielle while I finished my morning surgery.

Managers Talk

After a round of chit-chat and gossip about colleagues, Danielle and I sat together with the nurses to discuss more serious matters. Primarily, we talked about the communication between the HQ and the ship. Most of it took place via e-mail. For urgent matters the medical department had access to a satellite phone. That was not the issue. The concern was who to speak to on the other end of the phone, especially after-hours. Patients fall ill during all times of a day or night. Organizing medical care at 2 am was often not only difficult and time-consuming but also often frustrating. Even when calling dedicated crisis lines, I heard just a tape recording. That meant

I had to find alternative ways to arrange for emergency medical care, such as talking to the US Coast Guard. Danielle's solution for the problem was to e-mail her all the numbers which were not answering calls after-hours and she would "look into the issue" – whatever that meant.

Another topic we discussed was the quality of the medical facilities we utilized in the ports of call. They varied significantly, ranging from unusable (meaning dangerous) to pretty good (almost US standard). I had identified issues concerning a particular clinic on one of the smaller islands which was part of the *Jubilee's* itinerary. Doctors on other ships, who also used this facility, shared my concerns. And many of them, including myself, tried to avoid using their services as much as possible. Then again, in some instances there was no choice and we had to use this clinic. I suggested that Carnival should contract another clinic in that area. Danielle didn't promise anything, but agreed to minimize the use of the facility for the time being (which was what we were doing anyway – so I got another typical manager answer).

Main Blvd, Cozumel, Mexico

Then she surprised me when we discussed another matter closer at hand. I explained the problems we had with the Cozumel Medical Centre (CMC). In general, I found commutation with my colleagues at that clinic quite difficult. Not that they didn't speak English – they did – but they were very difficult to get hold of when phoning the clinic. It was often vital to speak with the physician who had treated the particular patient (predominately guests). I needed to know what was going on in order to make a judgement whether to allow them to return to the ship to sail with us. I couldn't rely on the word of the guests; they would tell me ANYTHING to come back onboard.

Getting hold of medical personnel of the CMC was therefore vital, but particularly difficult. So, I lamented my concern to Danielle. This time she took a no-nonsense approach to the problem. She suggested to visit the CMC right away to discuss the problems face to face with the doctors there.

Together with Sonia, the lead nurse, we made our way to the CMC. It was around noon when we left the *Jubilee* and stepped onto the quay. We were greeted by steaming hot air and a stinging sun. Fortunately, it was just a short stroll along the pier to the taxi rank. And after a 15-minute drive we arrived at the main entrance of the CMC. The clinic was surprisingly small, but modern and clean. For the first time I actually saw the place to which I had sent so many patients – guests and crewmembers alike.

Invitation or a (Little) Bribe?
Danielle had announced our visit just half an hour beforehand by phone. We were greeted by the wife of the medical director. Her name was Jenny, a delightful blonde American woman. She gave us a tour through the clinic, which was set up as an ER (Emergency Room) with a

few beds in the back for patients who had to stay a little longer. The rooms were all air-conditioned and clean (not a universal thing in Mexico). The clinic also had a laboratory and x-ray facilities. It had a small operating room to conduct minor surgery (i.e., stitching lacerations) or diagnostic procedures (i.e., endoscopy). It had even a CT scanner - well kind off… the scanner worked sometimes and sometimes it didn't. Jenny was honest enough to admit that the scanner was out of action during the time of our visit. My thought was: *Let's hope that nobody sustains a serious head injury in Cozumel until that thing is fixed.* In any case, the purpose of the CMC was to treat minor medical conditions and to stabilize critically ill patients to a level that they could be transferred to a hospital. The clinic was staffed with emergency doctors around the clock and specialists could be called in if needed.

Finally, we met the medical director of the clinic, Dr. Hernandez. He was a true Mexican with dark brown skin and Latin American complexion. Nevertheless, he spoke flawless English. He told us that he spent a lot of time in the States to attend medical conferences and courses. I suppose he wanted to give us the impression that his clinic has (almost) US standards. We sat down to discuss the problem of the fitness to sail and the communication issue between us doctors. Dr. Hernandez understood our concerns and he promised to instruct his doctors to provide medical reports with a clear recommendation on whether a patient was fit to sail or not. *Well, we will see if that will happen*, I thought. Nevertheless, he also gave me his cell phone number and his e-mail address with the offer to contact him if any problems arose. He was clearly anxious to please us and I was not surprised - given that we (and other cruise ships) gave him plenty of business. His invitation to meet for dinner again may have been driven by the same motivation – who knows? Still, we made arrangements for Danielle, the nurses and me to meet with him and his wife in a fancy restaurant in the evening. Thus, we were in for a jolly good night – provided all would be quiet on the medical front.

Tuesday, 7th of May 2002
Cozumel, Mexico

The Ship – the Refuge
The *Jubilee* was again moored at the quay in Cozumel. It almost felt like coming home whenever we were there. And that was not surprising, given that all the cruises we were running past this port of call – whether it was a three- or four-day run.

Restaurant garden, Cozumel

In the evening, I went out to have dinner onshore with Shree, the paymaster. The restaurant was just a quick taxi ride away from the quay. We settled for a table in the garden, which had a magnificent setting with lush and exotic plants and parrots in the trees. The place had been recommended by another crewmember. It was supposed to serve authentic Mexican food and not the tourist crap which could be found everywhere around Cozumel. The beginning of the dinner was promising. We started with a margarita which was served in a swimming pool sized glass and watched the golden sunset on the horizon. The temperature dropped to pleasant levels and life felt exceedingly good at that moment. And I truly deserved the treat after a hard and stressful working day.

Just a few hours earlier a passenger in his 60s had been brought to the infirmary by his relatives. This gentleman was complaining of chest pain. He was known to have heart problems, had had several heart attacks and two bypass operations. So far so good, but here comes the interesting bit of the story. He decided to go for a horse ride in the midday heat. Being exposed to the relentless sun and riding across the dry land of Cozumel was his idea of fun. Of course, he forgot to take some water, so he was very thirsty during his trip. After just an hour or so he got chest pains. So he decided to return to the ship to "get checked out."

Well, judging by the man's story, I assumed that he had become severely dehydrated and exhausted. I guessed that he had an angina attack or even another heart attack. He should have known better. With his past medical history, he should had gone to a hospital rather than back to the ship. But he did the typical thing guests did over and over again. No matter what happened to a guest onshore: a car accident, broken bones, whatever, they all came back to the ship to be cured by the ship's doctor. None of them appreciated that we were NOT a hospital, just a small clinic with limited capabilities. Nevertheless, we had an ECG machine (Electrocardiogram) in the infirmary. An ECG traces the electrical activity of the heart and can tell a doctor if there is something wrong with it. And bingo, the trace revealed that he had an inferio-lateral infarct, meaning a BIG heart attack. Of course, we had to call an ambulance and he was transferred to the local hospital where he should have gone to in the first place.

No Way!

After he had gone, I went for dinner to the nice restaurant. Soon it was time to return to the ship. At the gangway I was informed by the security officer that I needed to contact the purser's office immediately. The purser told me that the hospital had rung and tried to contact me. Hence, I phoned back and spoke with one of the doctors there. The conversation went as follows: "Hi doctor, you sent us a gentleman earlier today. He wants to come back to the ship," said the doctor. "But he had a big heart attack," I replied. "Yes, but he refuses to have any treatment here. He wants to travel back to the US on your ship. I just want to check whether that is alright with you." I couldn't believe my ears and gave him my answer which contained just two words: "No way!" "I thought you might say that," said the doctor on the other end.

My immediate action after this telephone conversation was to inform security at the gangway that this passenger was NOT to be allowed to board the ship under ANY circumstances. And if he tried to board, I should be notified immediately.

I had learnt that preventing boarding of ill passengers was vital. In the past, some of them had sneaked back onboard and could not be found before sailing. They were not in their cabins and requests via the PA system to present themselves to the infirmary were ignored. Once we were at sea, they came to the ship's clinic and I had to deal with their mess. That was one of the major challenges I faced as a ship's doctor. But I had found a simple solution: just deny them boarding in the first place. Sounds hard, but it was the right thing to do – for everybody concerned.

Being a Penguin

It was the second day into a cruise. And as I had mentioned before, that day featured always a "formal night". There was only one during a journey but they were scheduled for each and every cruise. It had become a (boring) routine for me.

A formal night started for me around 6 pm, after the last patient of my afternoon surgery had left the infirmary. I then migrated to my cabin to groom myself: taking a shower, shaving and all that. Next step was to dress up. I got into my formal uniform, consisting of black tuxedo trousers, a black waistcoat and a white dinner jacket, garnished with a bowtie. After that I had changed from a doctor into a penguin.

At 7:40 pm at the latest I made my way via the Promenade Deck towards the Atlantic Lounge. During formal night the guests were encouraged to dress up as well for that occasion. I have to say that most of them made an effort. Some of the women went through a lot of trouble and looked just breath-taking. But other guests didn't bother. I could always observe a broad spectrum concerning the dress code. It ranged from t-shirts and flip flops to men in tuxedos and women in fashionable evening dresses.

Ship's doctor in formal uniform

I usually entered the Atlantic Lounge around 7:45 pm. That lounge was the theatre of the ship. It had a stage and the seating stretching over two levels (decks) of the ship. It was the place where the entertainment acts happened, mostly dance shows and Bingo nights. But the second night of every cruise was reserved for the formal night to introduce the senior officers of the ship. The orchestra played popular songs while the auditorium filled up with guests. I headed for a special spot on the right side of stage where all the senior officers gathered. The finger food and the drinks offered there were of course free for us as we were still on duty. I never bothered about either. I was just eager to get done with the event. Each senior officer had his two minutes of fame on the stage. In the beginning I had a fair bit of stage fright. But after a while the whole routine became annoying rather than exciting. However, it was part of my duties as a ship's doctor and I had to attend.

The same procedure was repeated during every formal night. It was down to the cruise director to get onto the stage and kick off the show. First, he made a compliment to the crowd: how nice the ladies looked and how nice they had dressed their man (ha, ha). Then he announced that it was time to meet the senior officers of the ship and each of us had to come onto the stage. The DJ played the melody of M*A*S*H when I appeared. But there was a strict order.

The first to join the cruise director on the stage was the chef de cuisine (he was from Jamaica). Then the head of the housekeeping department (also from Jamaica) appeared, followed by the food and beverage manager (from Poland). Next in line were the chief purser and the hotel director (both from the US). After them the staff chief engineer, the chief engineer and staff captain (all from Italy) climbed onto the stage. My place was in between the chief purser and the hotel director. And there we were: standing in a nice line in our black and white uniforms like penguins. With a big fanfare the captain, the master of the vessel, came to join us on the stage. He welcomed the guests onboard the *M/S Jubilee* and then he guaranteed that, "this cruise will be the best ever". Then some music played as we left the stage. That was it; the "Penguin Parade" was over.

Dinner was Duty

As a cloud of white uniforms all senior officers, including myself, disappeared into the stairwell for crew. Only handful of us walked straight towards the officer's mess, where the captain's table was laid for the official dinner. To attend this event was actually part of the duties for all department heads. For that reason, I was expected to appear. Any absence needed some sort of reasonable excuse. Some of the senior officers were frequent attendees, for instance the hotel director Fred. Others, such as the chief engineer, were frequent absentees. (He probably preferred to "trawl" for female guests on the Promenade Deck.)

Bar on Promenade Deck

Personally, I found attending the dinner had some advantages. It was not exactly fun to sit around the captain's table in the stuffy atmosphere. Still, it was often enlightening to listen to what was said during the meal. Time and again I was able to hear of what actually was happening on the ship. On occasions, I even got snippets of information regarding changes and developments within the company. Sometimes we were joined by visitors to the ship, like representatives from Lloyds Register, contractors or people from Carnival HQ. These people were onboard for a few cruises to perform special tasks, such as installing equipment, implementing new policies or conducting inspections.

I found it always refreshing when a new face joined the table. It provided an opportunity to meet a different person and not just the usual crew. It also ensured that the language spoken was English. All Carnival Sea Officers onboard (including the captain) were from Italy. They frequently switched to their mother tongue during conversations with each other. That happened especially when we were joined by their family members. During those gatherings I truly felt out of place and that was not only owing to the fact that I didn't understand a word of what was said. In addition, I found the increased noise and wild gestures which came with the Italian language quite disconcerting. In those situations, I frequently "remembered" that I had to review a sick patient in the infirmary and made my escape from the dinner table.

My beloved Lido Deck

That morning I decided to have breakfast on Lido Deck to enjoy my favourite morning food: French toast with maple syrup. While I was munching the sweet sloppy toast and slurping my milky coffee, I realised that I was already halfway through my six-month contract. *Hm, what shall I do next?* I asked myself. Go home? Thinking of it, I actually had no home at the time as I had dissolved my residency in the UK. But my sister in Germany surely would provide me with a room for a while. Or I could see my friends in Australia again. Maybe I should visit some of my former colleagues in England. Well, I still had plenty of time to ponder about that matter as I had another three months to go.

Bar on Lido Deck

In any case, there was no time left to muse about a vacation since I had to go to work. My morning surgery turned out to be an interesting one as I came across an unusual case. A crewmember, aged 26, came to see me complaining of chest pain. An ECG done on the young man suggested a heart attack, which was extremely unlikely, given his age. What I needed was an expert opinion. Via the satellite phone I contacted the HQ in Miami. They instructed me to send a copy of the ECG via email, so it could be forwarded to a cardiologist.

Shore-side support regarding medical issues had always been quite good – with some exceptions. And even more importantly, it didn't matter what time of day (or night) a problem arose. Someone from the medical department at the HQ in Miami was always available to discuss complicated cases with me. And in most instances a solution was found, such as getting an expert opinion or sending the patient to an appropriate facility onshore. In desperate situations a medical evacuation was organized either by boat or (more often) by helicopter.

That morning I spoke to a cardiologist from Miami via the satellite phone. He had seen the ECG and recommended keeping the patient on a cardiac monitor for observations. The *Jubilee* was due to dock at Grand Cayman Islands the next day. There the patient could be send to the hospital for further investigations.

Having received clear guidance, I was able to leave the infirmary. It was time for my lunch, so I headed back to my treasured Lido Deck. I preferred to have my meals up there instead of in the crew mess. It was not the food that lured me to that place, but the atmosphere. Having a meal there felt like being on a vacation (well, almost, as I was constantly conscious that I was on call – my pager was always ready to go off). However, I enjoyed to sit on a sunny deck for my meals. Sometimes fellow officers or the nurses joined me there. Despite wearing a snow-white uniform and being clearly identifiable as a doctor, the guests tended not bother me. Nonetheless, some of them were brave enough to engage me in a conversation. That could be a good or bad thing. At times I met really interesting people there. But others just asked me stupid questions like: "Do you get a lot of people with seasickness?" Or worse: "I have this bad back pain…" If that happened, I withdrew from the encounter rather quickly, mumbling something about a medical emergency.

Art or Knick-Knack?

After lunch I usually had about two hours to enjoy myself. I often strolled along the decks, just to see what was going on. While I passed the Terrace Lounge, I noticed a lot of artwork displayed on the seats and tables. Upon entering I was offered a glass of (free) champagne, which I declined. I was in uniform and seeing the ship's doctor drinking in broad daylight wouldn't look good. So, I sipped a glass of orange juice instead while browsing through the artwork. There were cartoons on display, and I recognized Bugs Bunny and the Roadrunner.

Painting by Peter Max

All drawings were supposedly originals, produced for the cartoons (according to the attached certificates). There were also paintings by Peter Max. His works were incredibly colourful but not really artistic (in my eyes). To top off the cheesiness, I found sports jerseys with autographs of baseball or basketball players which were also for sale. Well, actually none of the stuff was for sale; it was part of an art auction. All the items I could see there in the lounge were due to be given to the highest bidder. The event was a concession and not run by Carnival. Actually, the same applied to the hairdresser's saloon and the gift shop. Even the golf pro onboard had a concession and his income depended on how many people joined him for a lesson on the ship or for a game onshore. The people who ran these concessions were kind of a crossbreed: not really crewmembers, but not guests either. It just so happened that they conducted their business on a ship. As patients I treated them free of charge while they were onboard. But they were required to fund any treatment onshore themselves (or via a health insurance). That made my life at times somewhat difficult. Quite often it was down to me to acquire some sort of funding for their hospital appointments. Regular crewmembers were in a better position as Carnival paid for all medical expenses which incurred onshore.

I left the art auction before the bidding began since I had to conduct my afternoon surgery. And afterwards I was expected to attend the formal night – again. It had become a repetitive procedure. First the Penguin Parade, followed by the dinner at the captain's table. Afterwards, I often went with some of my fellow officers for a stroll along the Promenade Deck. For the night of that day, I planned to meet with the nurses to have a drink at the Smugglers, a cosy bar where Mandy and her husband Robert performed. I got to know them quite well as we played golf together during our shore leave. Robert had managed a building company in the past. Unfortunately, his enterprise went bust so he made his hobby, playing music and singing, his new profession. Later Mandy joined him, first as a musician, then as his wife. They were "doing the ships" (performing on cruise ships) already for some years. Their repertoire consisted mainly of Country and Western music – cover versions only. In between their songs they cracked a few jokes. On the whole their show was aimed towards a more mature audience. I actually liked their act. So, what does that imply??

Saturday, 18th of May 2002
Tampa, Florida, USA

Gator Golf

Another "Tampa Day". The *Jubilee* had arrived at our home port Tampa and it was my day off. I had planned a grant day out with the usual suspects. Members of that gang were the musicians Robert and Mandy and Sonia, one of the nurses. At 7:30 am I got a wake-up call from Mandy: "Are you up doc?" My breakfast consisted of a quick coffee and a small croissant. At 8:00 am all of us gathered at the gangway, eager to leave the ship. Together with many other crewmembers we waited for a window to open – a short time period during which crewmembers were allowed to go onshore. Finally, security got the radio call from the bridge: "Crew window open for five minutes". Off we went, storming down the gangway towards freedom. What followed was a short walk along the quay towards a multi-storey car park where Robert kept his car.

Westfield Shopping Centre, Tampa

First, we drove to a shopping mall for a large breakfast and a little shopping. Then, around 10 am, we were all on a golf course. Playing golf in Florida was quite different from playing the game in England. Peak season is winter because it is still warm (but not hot) in the sunshine state and cold in the rest of the US. When we were there, it was stinking hot with temperatures well over 100°F (38°C). And then there was the humidity of at least 80 percent. That was the real killer. It makes you sweat without doing anything – never mind playing golf.

At least we didn't have to walk around in the heat. The use of a golf cart was compulsory on the course. It is not only easier, but it also speeds up the game – a typical American approach. Time is money! On the first hole the player had to hit the ball over a water hazard. I was convinced that there were plenty of balls in this little pond – including quite a few of mine. However, the greatest dangers on that golf course were not the water hazards or the sand bunkers, but alligators. Rangers patrolled the course frequently and gave warnings like: "There is a big gator on the 7th hole." Sometimes it was wiser to leave a ball that had landed near the water. I preferred to lose a golf ball rather than an arm or leg.

On the 5th hole I had a great drive off the tee but then disaster struck. The next stroke catapulted the ball right into an area of dense grass. To find the ball I was in need of the support of my fellow golfers who helped me to find the tiny white thing. We were all together in that game after all. The aim was not to win the US Open – just to have fun.

Ship's doctor taking a swing, Tampa

After three hours of golf in the scorching sun we were ready for a big, big drink. So, we treated ourselves to a huge glass of beer at the "Schnitzelhaus". The name said it all: it was a German restaurant or, to be more precise, it was what Americans *think* Germany is all about. The interior was decorated with pictures of mountains, old farmhouses and people in "Lederhosen" (leather trousers). The tables were made of sturdy dark wood and covered with blue and white chequered tablecloths. Everything had been done to make you think that you were not in Florida but in Bavaria. And that was the disturbing bit. In wide parts of the US, Germany equals Bavaria, which is in fact just a small part of Germany. Nevertheless, the beer, served in half litre glasses, was great and so was the meal: sausages with "Sauerkraut" (fermented white cabbage).

From Shore to Ship
But even the best meal had to come to an end. There was just time for a brief stop at the post office to check my mailbox and then we had to drive back to the ships' terminal. On the way to the *Jubilee* we passed the crew centre on the pier. Well, crew centre is probably a bit of an overstatement. It was just a long row of tables with phones on it under a gazebo. From there, overseas phone calls could be made cheaply so it was a busy place when a ship was in port. Languages from all corners of the world could be heard. For that reason, privacy was not a problem - as long as the immediate neighbours of a caller didn't understand the language spoken. Next to this long phone table were stands which sold stuff that crewmembers typically need, such as suitcases and padlocks. The stalls were just folding tables in front of a van covered by an awning. These covers were badly needed as protection against the ever-present sun (and the very occasional rain) in Florida.

None of us had the time for a phone call or to shop. Mandy and Richard needed to get ready for their gig that night and Sonia and I had a surgery to run in less than an hour. Thus, all of us headed straight towards the gangway. The swipe of my ID through the electronic reader was answered with a "ping", which indicated that all was fine, and the computer had recognized that I was back onboard. A nasty buzz meant that there was something wrong and I had to see the security guard. When that happened, security frequently instructed me that my presence was required somewhere on the ship. Often a sick patient was already waiting in the infirmary for me. Or I had to see the captain or chief purser to help to deal with some sort of (mostly unpleasant) incidence. That day I was lucky, and a friendly "ping" sound had greeted me at the gangway. I rushed to my cabin for a quick shower to wash off the sweat and dust from my round of golf. Clean and refreshed, I changed into my uniform, picked up my two-way radio and pager, and then made my way to the infirmary. There, the nurse on call filled me in on what had happened during my absence (I always hoped for nothing). I then walked up to the bridge to sign the logbook, stating that all was in order and the medical department was ready to sail.

After signing the logbook, I always enjoyed lingering on the bridge for a little while. Before departure US regulations stipulated that all passengers had to participate in an emergency drill. First, they had to assemble at the muster station (the place on the ship to meet in case of emergency). From there they were guided by a crewmember to the embarkation station (the location of their lifeboat). With a bright red life vest around their necks the guests looked like sheep following a shepherd.

On the bridge, M/S Jubilee

Right on time at 4 pm the lines were cleared and under the direct command of the captain the ship was taken out of the harbour. It required a delicate manoeuvre with only a few centimetres to spare between the quay wall and the ship's hull. While the ship slipped slowly out of the harbour, I frequently had a chat with one of the guys from the coastguard. Since 9/11, two or three coastguard officers remained on the bridge until the ship reached the open sea. Personally, I wasn't sure what they could do in case of a terrorist attack on a cruise ship but at least their presence made all of us on the bridge feel a bit more secure. On occasions I also had a few words with Santo, the first officer. He was always good for a friendly chat. However, I had to be sensible and not interfere with his ability to do his job. In fact, most of the time I was just happy to watch the action on the bridge and to absorb the atmosphere of composed professionalism. Orders were given and equipment handled. Some of the action made sense to me, others not. I was a medical officer and not a naval officer, after all. Nevertheless, I learnt a lot about seafaring.

Around 4:30 pm at the latest I had to go do down to the infirmary. For the about half hour, I was occupied with "exciting" tasks such as reading medical reports, reviewing laboratory results and checking e-mails. At 5 pm sharp, the ship's infirmary was opened for patients. On home port day I usually saw only a few crewmembers and the odd guest who had managed to find the infirmary within the first hour of the cruise. A common story was that of forgotten medication. For example, an elderly lady came with a request because she had forgotten her blood pressure medicine. Asked what she was taking, she answered: "A small pink tablet, doctor". It always amazed me that patients expect that a doctor would know what medications they take by just describing the size and colour of a tablet. Nevertheless, somehow, I always worked out what they need. The next question was whether we had it onboard. Usually, I was able to prescribe an appropriate substitute. But sometimes nothing equivalent was available. However, most of the medication requested was not a matter of life and death. And the patient was safe enough to do without it for the three or four days of the cruise.

The infirmary closed its doors around 6 pm. Every second home port day I called for a meeting of all the infirmary staff after closure. The matters discussed arose mainly from the captain's meeting or from my communication with the headquarters in Miami. It was also a forum for the team to voice any concerns or discontent. Fortunately, there was generally none of that. The small medical team, the three nurses and I, were on the whole a happy bunch.

After the meeting I was ready for my dinner – and the odd emergency call. But I always hoped for the best.

Ship's terminal entrance, Tampa

Thursday, 23rd of May 2002
Tampa, Florida, USA

The Boss is Here!
The days when the *Jubilee* was in Tampa, our home port, were usually days off duty for me. But that Thursday it was not possible to enjoy myself in town. Instead, I had to remain onboard to wait for a meeting with Steve. Everybody in the infirmary team was informed that he would be coming onboard. The question was: why? He was the medical director of Carnival Cruise Lines and effectively our boss. But it was unlikely that he made his way from the other side of Florida just to have a chat with us. Certainly, something was afoot. Expecting the boss for a meeting is always unsettling.

At 9 am I got a phone call from the captain. "Steve is with me. Would you like to join us for a meeting?" Of course I would! I went up to the captain's quarters. Over a cup of coffee and some Danish pastries we sat around a table to discuss medico-maritime issues such as helicopter evacuations, medical emergency procedures and crewmembers' welfare. We talked about how to streamline policies and how to make the work of the medical team safer and more efficient.

After more than an hour of intense discussions, Steve and I left the captain's cabin and walked along the Lido Deck. By then it was mid-morning and the deck was virtually empty. The guests from the previous cruise had left and the passengers for the next one were not expected to come on board before 2 pm. We made ourselves comfortable in an empty espresso bar to have a "heart to heart chat". Steve began the conversation with an evaluation of my performance as a ship's doctor. I had had to deal with challenging cases and difficult evacuations. Steve reported to me that HQ and he were of the opinion that I had done a "pretty good job". That's probably the highest praise one can get from management in the US. However, there was some icing on the cake as I was offered another contract. At that moment I felt rewarded for all those sleepless nights and hard work during the past months. I had learnt that a cruise ship is a very challenging environment to work in, but it appeared that I had managed (somehow) to execute the duties of a ship's doctor reasonably well.

After this affirmation of my abilities, I felt encouraged to mention a dispute with my current lead nurse. A few days earlier, I had a disagreement with her concerning clinical care. I am always happy to discuss matters of medical management with anybody, including nursing staff. But at the end of the day, it is the doctor who takes the responsibility for the health of the patient and therefore he or she should have the final say. In this instance, I had clashed with my lead nurse as she didn't agree with my choice of medication. It was a kind of a classic clash: doctor versus nurse. Steve was smart enough not to take sides but instead tried to mediate. He explained to me that the particular nurse was trained in New Zealand and that the nurses there work far more independently than in other countries. Still, he assured me of his support if an ongoing problem were to emerge and he reminded me that he or his deputies were contactable at the HQ in Miami 24/7 (meaning 24 hours a day, 7 days a week = always).

America – the land of lawyers, Tampa

Cool or Cruel?

Waiters began to appear to get the café ready for the guests who were due to arrive soon. Steve looked at his watch and I could feel that he wanted to finish our tête-à-tête. But there was one further subject I needed to discuss with him. It concerned my second nurse, Lora. She had made repeated mistakes and was forgetful. On one occasion she almost gave the wrong dose of IV (into the vein) medication, thus endangering the patient. With that incident she had crossed a red line for me. I had already spoken with Steve about her over the satellite phone and we had decided not to let her work unsupervised for the time being. Still, that was not a solution. I wondered what HQ's final decision was regarding her. Steve told me quite frankly that she had to go. Her replacement would arrive in a week's time. Then he asked me: "Do you want to tell her or shall I?" At the time I felt that "throat cutting" (US management jargon for a dismissal) was a job for him as the medical director rather than me and he agreed.

It then was time for Steve to leave the ship. He went back with me to the infirmary to say goodbye to the nurses. He was sweet to all of them, including to Lora. He asked her in a casual way to accompany him on his way out towards the gangway, which she did. Later I heard that he delivered the news of her dismissal while they walked the corridors of the ship. I think that was pretty cool – or cruel – depends on how one looks at it.

Although there were good reasons to fire that nurse, I did feel a bit guilty and uneasy about her dismissal. That day I was unable enjoy my home port day routine. However, I did my usual shopping, checked my mailbox and had my coffee at the Hyatt Hotel anyway. I wondered how Lora would behave during our usual team meeting in the evening. To my surprise, she was cool as a cumber. She didn't display any sign of nervousness or remorse. Well, maybe she was contemplating how to sue Carnival. We all were working for an American company after all. And America is the land of lawyers.

Tuesday, 29th of May 2002
Onboard M/S Jubilee, Caribbean Sea

Encounters

A few days earlier I had had lunch with Sonia, the nurse and Shree, the paymaster. We were sitting on the open deck, enjoyed the fresh air, sunshine and a free meal. Then out of the blue one of the cooks left the buffet and came to our table. He addressed me with a little speech, thanking me for the medicine I had given him. He told me that he felt so much better and then he asked me if he could do anything for me. I felt embarrassed because I couldn't even remember what I had done for him. So many people were going through my infirmary, it was difficult to remember them all. Of course, some of them one never forgets – for good or bad reasons. Nonetheless, this grateful crewmember was sure to make up for the next 100 unreasonable, ungrateful or right-out rude patients.

Patients from the US were often quite challenging (to be polite about the description of their demeanour). Most of them were looking for a quick fix. If given the choice of changing their behaviour or take a pill, they always would choose the latter. Even American doctors displayed that attitude. One day I had an ophthalmologist (eye doctor) in my consulting room. She demanded antibiotics for a simple cold. It was amazing how many people on the ship acquired coughs and colds due to of the cold air-conditioning. As a doctor she should have known that this kind of infection is mainly of viral origin, hence antibiotics are of no value. I tried to reason with her, colleague to colleague, but that made her only upset and angry. She finally stormed out of my consulting room and slammed the door so hard that the handle almost flew off. But I always followed my medical principals and would never prescribe medication inappropriately. Even if the CEO of Carnival Cruise Line had walked into the infirmary with inappropriate demands, I would not have given way (I think).

Some Appreciation (Sometimes)

A quite different clientele were crewmembers. I was their doctor for the duration of their contracts. Having access to good medical care was a privilege for most of them as a significant number of crewmembers came from under-developed countries. Also: Carnival paid for comprehensive medical care. That included medication and the consultations by specialists onshore.

Attending to them as their doctor had its challenges though. Their health concerns varied as much as the countries from which they came. It was often a challenge to get the concept of modern, science-based medicine across. And sometimes I wasn't sure whether the medication given to them was taken as prescribed.

Front desk, Infirmary, M/S Jubilee

Nonetheless, once I had earned their trust, they came to see me with all sorts of problems (medical and non-medical). And they were grateful for what I could do for them. One evening a cabin steward had an encounter with a sharp edge of a laundry trolley. He sustained a long and nasty cut to his leg, which I sutured with 10 or 12 stitches. As his injury was quite extensive, I cleaned and redressed his wound every day for almost a week. Luckily, the cut healed well, and I had almost forgotten about the incident. Yet, a few days later he came with his supervisor who translated for him as he only spoke little English. He thanked me whole heartedly for all what I had done for him and even gave me a little present. I almost burst into tears.

Occasionally (but really occasionally) I had grateful passengers. I remember a guest who came to the infirmary with a mysterious rash and a swelling of her face. My diagnosis was that she had an allergy of some sort and I treated her accordingly. Initially, she didn't respond to the treatment but after a few days she was significantly better. Two cruises later (that how we crewmembers calculated time – not in weeks) I received an e-mail from her. She reported that she had seen a specialist (Americans love to consult experts) who had confirmed my initial diagnosis. She told me that she was fine now, and she thanked me for all I had done for her on the ship. I made a print-out of her e-mail for a rainy day.

Some were more Equal
A very different type of patient were my fellow senior officers. The best way to describe them (in a politically-correct way) is to give them the attribute of "challenging". It always felt weird to treat the captain (sorry, master of the vessel). It was strange to ask him, technically my boss on the ship, detailed and sometimes embarrassing questions and then to touch him in intimate areas of his body, and finally I had to tell him what to do (or to avoid).

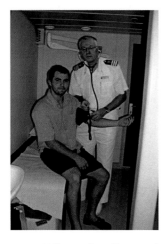

Ship's doctor consulting, MS **Jubilee**

Fellow senior officers such as the chief engineer, hotel director or chief purser were not as stressful to have as patients. They were my colleagues after all. However, the treatment they received was different from that for the average Joe. Not in regards to the medical care, but in terms of the courtesy they received. A senior officer never waited in the crew area but in a side room – if they waited at all. And I granted them the courtesy of seeing me outside surgery hours. In short, they had privileges. On the other hand, being a senior officer, I enjoyed privilege myself. I could join a shore excursion any time (without charge). If I attended a ship's restaurant, I always got the best table. I just could pop up at the hairdressers for a hair-cut without an appointment. And if I wanted to get something done, then I just had to ask the relevant department head and things happened quickly and without any fuss. So, the "VIP services" for my fellow senior officers were part of a two-way street.

Monday, 3rd of June 2002
Onboard M/S Jubilee, Grand Cayman Island

New Captain, New Tone
It was 6:15 am in the morning. The sun rose from the horizon and its red glow came through the windows. As I glanced through the glass pane, I just could make out the shore of the Cayman Islands in the distance. I had to spend that glorious morning on the bridge of the *Jubilee* – by order of the new captain. He had stipulated that the doctor had to be on the bridge during a medical evacuation. A little earlier I had spoken with the local authorities via the ship's radio. As arranged with them a tender (small boat) appeared from the shoreline and docked alongside the cruise ship. From high above I watched how my patient, lying on stretcher, was transferred onto the tender boat. A nurse was with him. She was assigned to accompany him to the shore and then all the way to the hospital in an ambulance.

Since the 28th of May a new captain was in command. He came with a new attitude and fresh ideas. Take the "Penguin Parade" for example. He demanded that all senior officers had to address the audience when appearing on stage. Some of my fellow senior officers lacked any enthusiasm for this. The housekeeping manager made a routine PR exercise out of his speech: "Welcome aboard the *Jubilee*. I hope we will exceed your expectations. Have a wonderful cruise!!!" Others were more creative, including the captain. He performed a little act with his chief engineer, which was as follows: The captain asked the engineer: "Who is driving the ship while I am here?" The engineer replied: "I don't know." "It's still me – on remote," announced the captain and presented his pager. Ha, ha, ha... I think my statement was somewhere in between the bone-dry correctness of the housekeeping manager and the joking of the captain.

It went something like this: "Good evening, ladies and gentlemen. As the ship's physician I *don't* want to see you. Don't take it personally. I am happy to see you in the gym or restaurant, but not in the infirmary of this ship. Stay healthy and have great cruise!"

After the successful evacuation and a routine morning surgery I had to perform a personal duty. I had to call a dear friend of mine – far, far away. It was his birthday and I always feel that it is important to stay in touch with people close to your heart and to maintain the friendship. However, being on the high seas made that task a bit more difficult. Talking to him was not just a matter of a simple phone call. I had to be in port to get to a phone. I could be naughty and use the satellite phone in the infirmary for a private call but I never did. Partly because I felt it was not right to do so, but also because I had the suspicion that the numbers dialed were recorded. The infirmary phone was for official business only and not for personal calls to Europe. Regular mail service was not an option to send a message, either. Even air mail was painstakingly slow. The best alternative to send my friend birthday greetings was to drop him an e-mail, an easy and cheap way to communicate. I had a computer with internet connection in my cabin and could fire off e-mails any time of the day. And I made ample use of that opportunity to ensure that the people at home didn't forget that I was floating around the Caribbean Sea.

Keeping in touch,
M/S Jubilee

Boredom Instead of Excitement

Life onboard the *Jubilee* had become a matter of routine – only interrupted by the odd medical emergency. My life followed the rhythm of the journeys: 5–5–4. Two five-day cruises followed by a four-day cruise and then the sequence repeated all over again. Weekdays had no meaning. I had Tampa, Grand Cayman, Key West or Cozumel days. And the whole crew had the same mindset. "I have had this headache since the last Cozumel, doc," would be the totally acceptable opening statement of a crew patient. Guests, on the other hand, still lived according to the days of the week and used them as a time reference. I then had to look on my desk calendar to find out what the current day of the week was. I had bought a calendar which displayed the week days in large letters. It enabled me to stay in tune with the time count onshore. And the funny cartoons on each day sheet kept me amused.

That calendar helped me to start the day with a laugh and I needed a bit of cheering up after the many weeks at sea. The excitement of working aboard a shiny cruise ship, floating around the Caribbean Sea, had vanished. Most of my life onboard was filled with dull routine and a bit of boredom had set in. Sometimes, I felt outright down and then I became tired and preferred to spend my free time in the cabin to sleep or doze on the couch. I talked to some of the more seasoned crewmembers about this. They told me that it was perfectly normal to feel that way. It was called the "midterm blues" and I was reassured that it would pass.

Over the past few weeks, I had started to watch a lot of television. Several programs could be received via satellite, yet all were coming from American channels. Nevertheless, I found some good shows to watch. *Law & Order, Frasier* and *The West Wing* were my absolute favorites. And there were televised sports events one could watch as well. At the time the NBA basketball playoffs were on – a big thing for every sports fan in the US. That year the *Los Angeles Lakers* had made it into the finals.

Fred, the hotel director, was from California and a great fan of that team. So he was never far away from a television screen when the Lakers were playing. One of their games ran even during the obligatory captain's dinner. Personally, I found the game rather boring to watch. Pass, pass, pass, score – team one. Pass, pass, pass, score – team two. That went on until a score of around 100 points. And then there were the interruptions in the form of penalties, free throws or time-outs. Most gaps were filled with annoying commercials. However, the Lakers played very well, which was not surprising. They had been the champions several times in the past. As for myself, I am a football man and therefore more interested in the football World Championships, which had started three days ago in South Korea and Japan. I was determined to find a way to watch the games of the German team – somehow.

Saturday 8th of June 2002
Cozumel, Mexico

Cozumel – the Chameleon

The *Jubilee* berthed at Cozumel every fourth or fifth day of our rounds across the Caribbean Sea – determined by the length of the cruise we were on. Although the destination was

geographically identical, the experience on the island was never the same. I had both exciting times and tedious days there, depending on my activity. Sometimes I didn't see Cozumel at all as I had to stay onboard. A few of those occasions were the days of compulsory training. So far, we – the infirmary staff – had four of those days. And two of them happened when the ship was in Cozumel. The instructors were flown in from the States and for a whole day the nurses and I were stuck in the infirmary listening to their presentations. One topic of our training was 'Paediatric Emergencies'.

We were told really scary stuff like having to insert a breathing tube down the throat of a baby who couldn't breathe anymore, or whacking a large needle into a child's leg to give fluids and medication. So far, we had been lucky and hadn't encountered any scenario where this sort of action was deemed to be necessary. Another training day we were taught how to take x-rays. That was time well spent as the quality of x-rays taken onboard the ship was often poor. I never took x-rays myself as that was a task the nurses had to perform. But it was useful to learn how to align the machine to the patient, how to calculate the correct level of radiation, how to use the chemicals to develop the film and much more. I was surprised to discover that taking a good x-ray is far more complex than I thought

Apart from these two training days the medical department had a lot of fun in Cozumel. Unsurprisingly, the island was awash with tourist traps such as bars and restaurants. Yet, the real charm of the island was found away from the drinks, music and food. There were lovely walks to discover which led to secluded beaches and lagoons. Even during wet weather, we were able to enjoy ourselves in Cozumel. It was pretty cool to get around the island in a 4-wheel-drive vehicle and to rush through huge puddles with mud splashing onto the wind screen. That was even better than a ride on a funfair.

Beach on the island of Cozumel

A Marriage of Convenience?
However, on that particular "Cozumel day" I was a lazy boy, just resting on a beach lounger near a hotel pool with a huge piña colada in hand. I mused over the little party we had in nurse Sonia's cabin a few days earlier. Her cabin had no windows and in dim neon light a handful of guests enjoyed cheap champagne and a few nibbles. The occasion was the wedding of two crewmembers, the golf pro Steve and a barmaid called Lina. The pro was an American citizen and Lina came from Lithuania. Since the opening of the Iron Curtain, a lot of crewmembers were recruited from Eastern European countries. Previously many staff members had been from South Asian countries such as India. Rumor had it that the company had changed their hiring policy to have more white skin onboard, as that was (allegedly) preferred by the guests.

Whether that was true or not, the girls from the Eastern European countries were candy for the eyes and I was not surprised that Steve had fallen for one of them. But the question arose as to whether the girl had married him or his Green Card, which comes with the marriage to a US citizen. For Lina, the marriage was a ticket to have a convenient life in the US, away from the poverty and political upheaval in her home country. At least Steve's parents seemed to be suspicious as they were not too happy about the marriage. The party was slow and full of awkward conversations. I left soon after I had conveyed my congratulations. May the newlyweds find happiness!

I enjoyed my afternoon at the hotel pool, but this was followed by a busy evening surgery. The *Jubilee* was scheduled to leave the port of Cozumel at midnight. About 15 minutes before departure, I appeared duly on the bridge to sign the logbook. Each department head had to sign it to indicate that everything was in order and that their section was ready to sail. Having signed for the medical department, I always enjoyed remaining on the bridge to watch the sometimes-hectic activities to get the ship ready for departure.

That night, part of the excitement was (again) missing guests. Now and then, crewmembers or passengers alike failed to reach the vessel in time for departure. Often the captain held the ship for a while, but eventually the ship had to sail. The port agent then dealt with the people left behind. Crewmembers were sent to the next port of call to re-join the ship but got a written warning. The consequences of missing the ship for guests varied, depending on the circumstances. Most re-joined the ship at the next port of call, or they flew home altogether. A few chose to join the next Carnival ship to sail home with. The *Jubilee* had its fair share of admitting stranded passengers. As for myself, I actually couldn't miss the ship. A passenger vessel can sail without the chief engineer, but NOT without the doctor, according to international regulations.

Saturday, 15th of June 2002
Tampa, Florida, USA

Being Onboard means being On-Call
That day in June was an unusual day for me: the ship was in home port but I remained onboard. Normally, I was one of the first to escape the ship's life and to enjoy the delights of Tampa. But that day I had chosen to remain in my cabin to watch a football game. It was not just any old game but a match between nations: Germany versus Paraguay. The football World Championships were on and Germany had made it to the final 16 teams. The Americans call football "soccer", as football means American football. Soccer has never been a big deal in the US. For that reason, none of the major American networks televised the championship games. But the captain was from Italy and he had ensured that the games were available on the ship's satellite television.

Ships Terminal, Tampa, Florida, USA

"My" (the German) team had played the night before (well, early morning to be precise, at 2:30 am). I had videotaped the game to watch it in the comfort of my cabin the following day when the ship was at home port. The game had not even reached the second half when the phone rang. The caller informed me that there was an emergency in the infirmary. A driver of one of the Carnival buses had cut his hand. I was a bit annoyed as I was not even on call but I was onboard and I suppose a doctor is on duty 24/7. So, I duly stopped the video and went down to the infirmary to attend to the disaster. The injury was actually pretty bad. The man had sustained a long cut to his hand when he had tried to mend something on the vehicle.

Before I started to stitch the cut, I warned everybody NOT to blab the score of the football game I had started to watch. After I had put in half a dozen of stitches into the guy's hand, I made my way back towards my cabin. I just prayed that I wouldn't encounter anybody who would yell out the score. Most Americans didn't give a damn about the football (soccer) championships but the European (and even more so the South American) crewmembers were mad about football. Luckily, I entered my cabin unchallenged and was able to watch the rest of the game undisturbed. The German team won 1:0 against Paraguay and "my" team reached the quarter finals. Hooray!

Another Throat Cut

During our last "Tampa Day" we had a change within the medical staffing. Linda, the most experienced nurse in my team had to go. I really felt sorry to see her leave. She was an excellent nurse with a sound judgement and flawless clinical skills. But there had been an incident which had led to her dismissal. One night she was called to see a passenger, who had a seizure. After the attack, the patient was stabilized and transported to the infirmary in a wheelchair to be seen by me, the ship's doctor. From my point of view, she made the correct decision but the relatives of the patient thought differently. They complained bitterly that she hadn't called the doctor to the cabin. (This would have made no difference to the treatment or outcome whatsoever).

The following morning, I had to write a report about the event and the captain called for a meeting with the hotel director and me. The case was discussed in detail. I defended Linda's actions as she had done the right thing. However, during the meeting I got the impression that guest relations were far more important than good medical care. Linda had the tendency to speak quite frankly with patients. Some would even say that she was downright rude on occasions and a few crewmembers were actually scared of her. During the meeting, I learnt that there had been complaints about her from guests and crew alike. The chief subject of the criticism was about her attitude, which lacked friendliness at times. Whereas the other nurse, Sonia, was pretty much the opposite. She was able to chat with everybody, no matter who they were. She had good social skills, which sadly were NOT matched by her clinical abilities.

The outcome of the meeting was to put the case to the HQ for a decision. From there the verdict came that Linda had to go. I suppose the "seizure incident" was a welcomed reason to get rid of an unpopular employee. But I lost a good nurse.

Monday, 17th of June 2002
Onboard M/S Jubilee, Grand Cayman Islands

What Next?

After my morning surgery, I had made myself comfortable in one of the deckchairs on the Promenade Deck. I took a glimpse over the railing and what I saw was a blue sky over blue water divided by the coastline of Grand Cayman. Several cruise ships close by were lying at anchor like the good old *Jubilee*. Tender boats whizzed like little bees from the ships to the small harbor to get passengers ashore. Robert and Mandy, the musicians, were due to appear any minute for an informal meeting. They have been working on Carnival ships for years. If anybody knew about routes, harbors and cruise ships then it was them. I needed their advice to answer an important question: Which ship should I join next? Steve, the medical director, had offered me another contract and I was asked to indicate on which ship I would prefer to serve. That raised a lot of questions. Each Carnival ship had a specific run, which was done over and over again. Cruises on a flashy ship to exotic destinations were tempting but I had to be practical. The ports of calls are a key issue. What facilities are available there? Do they have shopping centers, a post office, a bank? Should it be a small ship (to keep the workload down) or a large ship with two doctors (to share the burden)? Short cruises are better because the ship moors at the home port more often and a home port day is essentially a day off. Days at sea can be a drag as during those days I would be unable to transfer medical emergencies to shore.

Anchored Cruise Ships, Cayman Islands

After a long discussion with the couple, it emerged that the *Ecstasy* might be a good choice. It is a medium-sized ship which ran from the port of Los Angeles (good infrastructure). The three- or four-day cruises set out for Catalina Island (which has an acceptable hospital to deal with emergencies) and to Ensenada, Mexico (good to have some fun). Hence, to work on the *Ecstasy* sounded appealing and I decided to inform Steve accordingly. However, I had no clue what my chances were of getting onto that ship.

Cards & Golf
There was no lunchtime meeting that day – thank god! I still had enough from the last one just the day before. What was it about again? Ah yes, the evaluation report of the crewmember comment cards. That was one of these bright ideas from the management at the HQ. A questionnaire (called a comment card) was handed out to all crewmembers across the whole Carnival fleet. Even I had the pleasure of filling one out. I could rate the food and the friendliness around the ship. There were questions like: Are you aware of the Carnival philosophy? (Actually, I was not.) Does your supervisor respects you as an individual? Do you feel part of the team? And so on... Then thousands of these cards were evaluated and during that very lunch meeting the results concerning the *Jubilee* were presented – but only to the heads of departments.

Accordingly, I went to the meeting as the head of the medical department. The venue was the crew training center. That was an awful dull environment, a room stuffed with books, computers and a few desks. No food or drinks were allowed in there and so I missed out on my usual "meeting coffee". Caffeine intake usually ensures that I am in a good mood before (and hopefully during) meetings.

Fred, the hotel director, chaired the meeting and dished out the ratings. The staff captain had a low popularity rating. Well, that was not surprising as he was in charge of discipline. That made him the "bad guy" by default. Fred himself was rated higher. Maybe it had helped that he had attended a lot of social crew functions during the past few weeks. The infirmary was rated as a unit and not its individual members (and I wondered why). Anyhow, our services were rated a bit above average. The highest ratings were awarded to the chef for his food. The friendliness onboard the *Jubilee* was up from last year but still below the fleet's average...and on and on it went. Fred presented numbers for more than an hour. But there was no debate. Why was that rating up and the other one down? How could conditions be improved? There was no discussion whatsoever. In my opinion, the whole exercise seemed to be a ghastly waste of time.

Veranda Deck, M/S Jubilee

At the end of that meeting, I felt totally exhausted. With a last flicker of energy, I staggered to my cabin to slump my tired mind and body in front of the television. A recap of the US Open golf tournament was on. Tiger Woods had won it with his mighty driver and magic putter. That meant he was still on course for the Grand Slam – winning all four major championships within one year. He already had won the Masters in Augusta/Georgia in April and now the US Open. The next major golf tournaments he had to win were the British Open in July and then the US PGA competition in August. If he managed to do that, then he would enter the golf's hall of fame. Let's wait and see…golf is a strange game.

Tuesday, 18th of June 2002
Cozumel, Mexico

A Party with a Blow
Party time! Well, for the guests it was party time around the clock for the duration of a cruise, but not for us crewmembers. Except, last night was OUR night! A section around the main pool had been changed into an area "for crew only". I went to the party around 10:30 pm to fulfil my duties rather than to have fun. I was dead tired from an exhausting day. Still, as a department head I had to demonstrate that I am part of the team, part of the Carnival family.

The bars around the pool were enormously busy, which was no wonder as drinks were free for another half an hour. Tables next to the first aid point bent under the load of the food on them. Loud music swept across the deck, but only a few brave souls danced to the rhythm. Attendance was good, but most just stood around drinking and chatting. Occasionally a splash came from the pool when someone went down the waterslide. I recognized a few familiar faces. Fred, the hotel director, was there as well as the safety officer and most of the officers from the bridge. But I didn't see the captain.

Sonia spotted me and came over to tell that she had extended her contract and would stay on the ship for two more months. That was a big blow to our mutual plan to visit our musician friends Robert and Mandy in their hometown Montreal. The extension of her contact made that impossible and all my arrangements relating to the end my current contract revolved around that visit.

Water slide, M/S Jubilee

With her decision she had blown that idea out of the water – just like that. My feelings that night were a mixture of anger and disappointment. Well, one never knows what goes on inside a person. Maybe some people just pretend to be a friend to gain an advantage and Sonia certainly needed to keep me sweet. I was her boss, and she might have tried to compensate for her professional shortcomings. Perhaps the proposed joint visit to Montreal was just a scam. Or was I just getting paranoid?

Onboard a Booze Boat

Another day, another party. It was an idea of Shree, the paymaster on the *Jubilee*. It so happened that another Carnival ship, the *Paradise*, was docked at the same time and at the same pier in Cozumel that day. Subsequently, the idea was born to meet with Shree's friend, Ozzy, a fellow accountant on the *Paradise*. The plan was to go on a boat tour around the island. Sounded like a good idea at the time – except we ended up on a party boat. So, Ozzy, Shree and I were sitting on the open upper deck, slurping sweet pink tequila. Our ears were hammered with loud Latin music. The scene was set for a wild fiesta and, indeed, on the deck below us a bunch of people had already started to dance. Just a few minutes earlier the boat had moved away from the quay and had passed the *Jubilee* and *Paradise*. It was great to see the cruise ships from the outside as it meant I was off duty – although only for a few hours.

We had joined the boat around lunch time together with roughly 50 tourists. The vessel was basically a floating matchbox with two decks. All the action was below us, with a dance floor and the bar. The drinks were all complementary. Ozzy and Shree joined the fun on the lower deck, while I preferred to stay in the open to gaze at the coastline. As I sipped cheap tequila from my plastic cup, the boat passed crowded beaches and large hotel complexes. But between them I spotted untouched nature reserves with lush vegetation and rough cliffs. I doubted that many of the people below me noticed any of the beauty we passed. As the party progressed, the people got increasingly drunk, loud and wild. And I wondered why these individuals came to this part of the world in the first place. What is the point of traveling hundreds of miles to get onto an ugly boat to drink yourself silly? Well, I suppose there are many different ideas on how to enjoy life...

Testing a floating Motorbike

After a two-hour journey along the coast of Cozumel, the boat arrived at a beach resort where everybody had to disembark. Some passengers struggled to make it safely over the gangway and onto the beach. Well, that was not a surprise after all that drinking in the midday heat. The beach resort offered the usual services, such as a restaurant, bar and swimming pool. And it was also possible to hire diving gear, kayaks and sailing boats. Also available were Jet-skis which are basically motorcycles on water. I had never been on one of those but had noticed them rushing up and down almost every coastal strip in the Caribbean. I had always wondered what it would be like to ride one of these machines. And there and then was an opportunity to find that out. So, I checked it out: 50 bucks (US dollars) for 30 minutes – sounded ok to me. I asked Ozzy if he would like to join me on a ride. He wholeheartedly agreed. We got a life vest and instructions on how to handle the beast. To my surprise there were some rules, such as to drive only slowly near the coastline and to stay away from the swimmers' area. In the open water we were allowed to give it the full throttle. Ozzy asked me to do the steering for the first half. Thus, I climbed onto the front seat, which was a quite wobbly affair. Ozzy took the back seat and off we went towards the open water. Once there, I revved up the engine to maximum speed. Wow, the acceleration was awesome – it almost threw us from our seats. The spray hit my face as I tackled the waves.

Hired Jet Ski, Cozumel

It certainly was an incredibly bumpy ride. I had to hold the handlebars with a firm grip and had to be careful keep the balance in order not to capsize. A bright yellow plastic cord was wrapped around my right wrist. It was connected to a mechanism that would stop the engine if I fall off. That ensured that the Jet-ski does not move on without the driver. It was surprisingly exhausting to maneuver the floating bike and I was happy to hand the steering over to Ozzy. It took a little balancing act but then I was sitting safely in the back – a far more relaxing position. I left it to Ozzy to chase another Jet-ski. We outraced it – but at price. The casualty was my cap. It flew into the water and was never seen again.

Friday, 21ˢᵗ of June 2002
Key West, Florida, USA

Key West, my Love
We (the *Jubilee* and I) were in Key West again. I had planned to leave the ship ASAP – right after my morning surgery. I loved Key West. Why? I guess it was the atmosphere. While walking along the streets of Key West, my favorite occupation was to gaze at the people around me. Almost everybody looked relaxed and happy. Pedestrians strolled along the lanes and avenues leisurely, which was very different from other cities in the US where everybody seemed to be in a rush. Then again, Key West had the sunshine and plenty of places to relax. The town has probably hundreds of pubs, shops, cafes and restaurants and all provided an opportunity to unwind, to hang out. A lot of people let the time just go by – many were on holiday, after all.

Successor of Sloppy Joe's bar, Key West

I was not the only one who liked Key West. Ernest Hemingway was also a member of that club. His first visit to Key West was in 1928, when he stayed for only six weeks, but fell in love with the place. He later bought a big house where he lived with his first wife. Ernest had a daily routine: writing in the morning, fishing in the afternoon and drinking at Sloppy Joe's in the evening. He must have been a good customer for that bar. One of the toilets from Sloppy Joe's ended up in his garden. Hemingway had got hold of it during works in the bar's bathroom. He just loaded it on his shoulders, uttering: "So much of my money ran through this, so it's mine now." (Nice story, although it may not be true.)

Other famous men also found Key West appealing: Harry S. Truman, Dwight Eisenhower and John F. Kennedy – all of them were President of the United States of America. Truman was the first to come in 1946. He and other presidents lived in the "Little White House" when they were in Key West. The house is now a museum.

The Little White House, Key West

During that day in June, I strolled down Duval Street. It was THE street, where it all happened. Tourist buses, mini trains, motor scooters and open Jeeps were on the road. Countless people walked up and down the strip. Or they had a drink or some food in one of the many pubs, cafes and restaurants. But the most popular occupation was shopping. Duval Street had loads of shops which sold souvenirs and other useless knick-knacks.

Duval Street, Key West

It was hot day, but I could cope because it was not humid. I made my way to the "Southernmost Point of the United States", a major tourist attraction. There I joined the queue for a photo with the official sign. It was quite a wait since the photo-taking in front of me didn't seem to end. Jenny (or whatever her name was) took a photo of Johnny and then Johnny of Jenny. Then it was Frank's, Tony's and Mary's turn to have their picture taken in front of the big ugly concrete block. First as a group and then each of them had a snapshot in a more or less (they thought) funny posture. And then it was the turn of the next group…and then a couple…and then… After what seemed to be an everlasting wait, I decided not to bother anymore. I preferred to walk further along the coast to a snow-white pier. It provided a great view over the deep blue sea right up to the horizon with a radar station of the US Navy in sight. The navy plays a big role in this part of the States. Their ships and sailors could be seen pretty much everywhere around the Keys.

Wreck ahoy!
It finally happened: I got caught in one of the many tourist traps. A man wearing sailor's clothing from the nineteenth century was walking the streets of Key West, enlisting people to join the "wreckers". Actually, he was an actor who recruited tourists for the Shipwreck Museum. Still, I was intrigued and curious, so I got a ticket and entered the little museum. A film told the story of the wreckers, people who risked their lives to salvage shipwrecks. And in the "good old days" there were plenty of wrecks, thanks to hurricanes and reefs. A lookout on a tower would watch the coast. When the call "wreck ashore!" sounded, the master wrecker and his crew got into action, hurrying to be the first at the ship in distress. Each and every man (sorry, no girls) was prepared to risk his life in treacherous weather. The rewards were great if they managed to salvage the cargo of the wreck.

On the 28 August 1878 the *Isaac Allerton* sunk near the Florida Keys. The wreckers were successful and saved most of the ship's cargo, which was then – legally – sold ashore. It attracted a salvage award of $150,000 – a fortune at the time. At the end of the nineteenth century, salvage operations were a frequent event. During that period the whole city of Key West was thriving on it. Some wreck masters acquired significant wealth through their business. After watching the film, I strolled through the museum's exhibit area. On display were mostly artifacts from shipwrecks, such as bottles, candle holders and pieces of china. Finally, I made the short climb onto the "wrecker's watchtower". It provided an okay view – but not really breath-taking.

Time flew and after the visit to the museum I had to hurry back to the ship's terminal, where I joined a gigantic queue. Hundreds of people, guests and crew alike, were about to board the ship during the last few minutes before departure. I duly got in line. Crewmembers were not allowed to jump the queue anymore because it had caused resentment among the guests. But I didn't mind. I was sure that a lot of work was waiting for me in the ship's infirmary.

Thursday, 27th of June 2002
Cozumel, Mexico

Tourists: Blessing or Curse?
It was a lovely night. A balmy and gentle breeze caressed my skin. I stood at the ship's railing on the Lido Deck. The blinking lights of bars and restaurants on the shore could be seen in the distance. It was 10 pm and I had just signed the logbook on the bridge. The *Jubilee* was ready to leave Cozumel. The large ropes were pulled in and the ship began to move away from the quay before turning towards the open sea and speeding up. Soon the lights on the shore were reduced to little sparks and then total darkness surrounded the ship. It was one of those moments when I truly enjoyed being a doctor on a ship rather than in a dull office.

Cozumel at night

It had been a relaxing day. I took a taxi to the city centre of Cozumel right after my morning surgery. I wanted to see the new shopping centre that crewmembers were raving about. It was a fairly big complex for Cozumel, but quite small by American standards. However, it had all the customary facilities: cafes, restaurants, a chemist, plenty of shops, and even a cinema. Everything was shiny and brand new. It almost felt like being in the States. Just a few decades ago Cozumel had been quite a different place. I had seen some pictures of Cozumel at the local museum. They had been taken in the 1950s and showed just a few dusty roads and simple small houses, most of which didn't have electricity or running water, never mind air-conditioning. American tourists discovered Cozumel in the 1960s and from then on they came in ever greater numbers. And that's why many recent developments had happened on the island, including the brand-new shopping centre and the countless resorts and hotels. I had heard that a new a quay was planned for even bigger cruise ships. Is this all good or bad? I don't know. The tourists bring money which is desperately needed by the locals. But how many tourists can this little island take? Resources such as water and land are not infinite. Then again, does anybody care as long as the money keeps coming in?

Cozumel during the 1950s
(Google Images)

A few Happy Hours

I went to the shopping centre to treat myself to a movie. It was one of those rare occasions I could be exposed to some sort of culture, apart from the ship's dance shows and onboard comedians. An electronic program was displayed at the entrance of the cinema. Most of the movies were in Spanish of course. However, all American films were shown in the original version with Spanish subtitles, which made these movies suitable for me. I was not interested in all that crime and action stuff. A movie with the title *40 Days and 40 Nights* caught my eye. It was advertised as a satirical comedy. The next screening was in 45 minutes. That left enough time for a quick drink and a snack before the show. The movie told the story of a young man, working in an office in San Francisco. One fine day he takes a vow of celibacy for 40 days and 40 nights after an ugly relationship breakup. His co-workers create a betting pool on whether he would succeed – or not. The hero has to battle with all the temptations society has on offer plus the actions of unscrupulous bettors. They try to get him to break his vow by playing dirty tricks on him in order to win their bet. On top of all that he falls in love with a girl. That plot provided amusement for a good hour and a half. But at the end of the movie, I had doubts whether the film represented culture as such. Seeing the happy ending on the screen was also the end of my happy hours off the ship. It was time to catch a taxi to get back to the ship where undoubtedly a few patients were waiting for me.

Cozumel Ships Terminal

A few Memories

Around 6 pm the nurses and I made our way from the infirmary to the crew bar. There we met up with the musicians Mandy and Robert to celebrate the end of their contract. Having entertained the guests onboard the *Jubilee* for six months, they were due to leave the ship the next day. After a few drinks Mandy and Robert had to withdraw to their cabin as they still had a lot of packing to do. Hence the medical department was left to their own devices and we started to reminisce about a few memorable patients.

The saddest case we could remember was that of a cabin steward from Jamaica. He had come to see me complaining of blurred vision in his left eye. He had these symptoms for a few weeks. First, he thought it was just tiredness. Unfortunately, it didn't get better. Still, he hesitated to seek help from the ship's infirmary because he was afraid to lose his job if he reported sick. At the end it got so bad that he could hardly see out of his left eye. When I examined the eye, I noticed a paleness of his retina. I suspected a vascular (blood circulatory) problem. I excused him from all duties and sent him to a specialist. The ophthalmologist diagnosed a degenerative process, which basically means "it just happens". Sadly, the patient was right. He lost his job and had to sign off at the end of the cruise. Without a definite diagnosis there was no treatment for him, subsequently the outlook for this man was very grim indeed. He was an example of the dark side of life a doctor sees when practicing medicine. During my career I have seen many lives go down the drain.

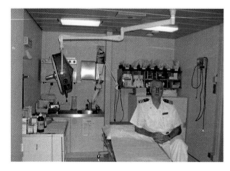

Treatment room, M/S Jubilee

Most of the memorable patients were guests. A few cruises ago a young woman got her finger trapped in a cabin door. That was one of the classic accidents on a cruise ship. She was lucky and no major damage had been done, although most of her nail came off (not a big deal, really). A perfect new nail would grow on that finger. But then the old nail had to be removed and the woman was an absolute drama queen. A river of tears came down her cheeks and she was adamant that she didn't want to lose her beautiful nail. She wouldn't even let me come near her to examine her finger more closely. Her boyfriend was not much help either. He just shouted at me: "You have to do something, doc! Help her!" After extensive negotiations we agreed to wrap her finger in a loose bandage. She promised to see her family doctor two days later once she was back home. I was fairly certain that by then the nail would have fallen off anyway. All that fuss for nothing!

And then there was an unforgettable night two weeks ago. Security called me at 4 am after a mass brawl in the disco. There was a long line of young men in front of the infirmary, all waiting to be examined. Some of them had cuts which I had to stitch. It was a long night (and morning) for me. Not only because I had to treat their injuries and to write the accompanying medical notes. I also had to produce an internal report for each case as the fight was deemed to be a critical security incident.

Another night proved to be equally stressful. I was called to the infirmary to see a young girl who had allegedly been raped. I could only do a basic examination but was not able to secure any evidence. The infirmary of a cruise ship was not geared to act as CSI (Crime Scene Investigation) laboratory. Upon our arrival in Tampa, the ship was sealed, and police officers interrogated everybody involved in the incident. That included also the medical staff as we had attended to the victim. Being questioned felt like taking part in *Law & Order*, an American crime series. The police officer who interviewed me had his badge hanging from breast pocket. He asked me a lot of tough questions, such as: What happened? When? What did you do next? …and so on. And I was just a witness – not the accused. Having been grilled for more than 30 minutes I left the room totally exhausted. Interestingly, Carnival sent its own investigator the same day. He was an ex-cop who asked me similar questions. And, of course, I had to write a long, long report about the whole thing.

To warn of a Warning

As matter of fact, I had to write a lot of internal reports. A frequent occurrence, which demanded an account of events, were falls onboard the ship. The floor around the swimming pools was especially dangerous. It was (understandably) wet around that area and therefore slippery. As a result, guests often fell around swimming pools. As the ship's doctor it then was my job to check them out. Frequently x-rays were taken to prove that they hadn't broken any bones. I never had a case of any serious injuries resulting from a slip on a deck. Nevertheless, many of the patients demanded a copy of my medical notes. I had no doubts that these individuals would see a lawyer once being home to determine whether they had a case to sue CCL (Carnival Cruise Lines). To reduce the number of accidents, signs were set up around the swimming pools to warn about the slippery ground. And guess what? One of the guests managed to walk into one of these signs and fell over. So, in a meeting I suggested we erect signs to warn about the signs. Sadly, my suggestion was not put into action.

Another frequent event was getting a call from security, usually in the small hours of the morning. The typical message was: "We have found an unconscious person in cabin so-and-so". Just a few days ago I was called to see a 15-year-old girl who was found in her bed, barely breathing. And, yes, she was drunk as a skunk. But I wondered what else she may have taken. We were sailing out of Mexico and she might have been shopping around there for drugs.

Just as I arrived on the scene, she started to vomit profusely. Thus, I had to insert a tube into her stomach to release the pressure and to protect her airways. Luckily, we were only a few hours away from our arrival in Tampa. I ordered an ambulance to the quay via satellite phone to transport the patient to the hospital as soon as the ship had docked. What a way to end a cruise! Many of the US kids were unable to handle the booze. The secret of staying in control lies in moderation. The nurses and I had to control our own alcohol intake strictly in order to be able to act professionally at any time. Even after a goodbye party in the Crew Bar!

Friday, 4ᵗʰ of July 2002
Tampa, Florida, USA

Chores First

That very day the *Jubilee* docked in Tampa, her home port, was a public holiday – Independence Day. The security arrangements were therefore strict. I had to endure several checks of my ID and bag before I was able to hit the streets of Tampa. Many shops and business were closed. Still, I was able to conduct my dealings. My post office box contained nothing exciting, just the BMJ (British Medical Journal) and statements from my American bank account. Another task, I had to do that day, was to book a room for my sister in a hotel downtown. She was scheduled to come over from Germany in two weeks' time to join me on the ship for a while. Since the regular shops were closed, I was forced to do my shopping in a drug store. Having done all my chores, I treated myself to a drink at the Marriott Hotel. I chose to sit at a table on the veranda, overlooking the marina with its yachts and sailing boats. The temperature was rather agreeable as the air had cooled down significantly after rain a few hours earlier.

Marriot Hotel and Marina, Tampa

As I slurped my Coke with rum, I found the time to reflect on the past cruise. It was a "Cozumel run" and I had finally taken a look at what was going on underwater. With about 20 other "divers" I sat in a submarine with large windows. It was truly magnificent to see the blue underworld. The fish living down there came in a great variety of shapes and colours. Curious dolphins swam past the window as the boat drifted along a reef. "Real divers" were easily identified. They were the figures that sent big bubbles towards the surface of the water. Personally, I preferred to stay dry and still be able to be with them in the same environment. Besides, I had seen enough diving accidents to appreciate the safety of a submarine.

Nasty Things happen (Even on a Ship)
What else had happened during the last cruise? More medical emergencies of course! In the early hours of the morning, I had to send a young girl to the Tampa General Hospital. She had a spectacular (actually very nasty) wrist fracture. The broken bone had pierced right through the skin and was sticking out. How had she done it? Falling off an upper bunk bed – drunk of course! Another memorable (and sad) case was that of my cabin steward. Three fingers of his right hand had got trapped in the frame of a heavy fire door and were badly injured. He was a very nice guy from Indonesia, always helpful, always friendly. Even when I saw him in the infirmary to attend to his fingers he was smiling. I didn't know what to tell him. His injury was pretty bad, and I wasn't sure whether all of his wounded fingers could be saved. The good news was that the next port of call was the Cayman Islands, a place with reasonably good medical facilities. I just had to keep him medically "afloat" until he could be seen in a hospital. I got the bleeding under control and gave him antibiotics to prevent any infection. Of course, he required big doses of analgesia to control his pain. I never heard from him again, but I truly hope that he is alright.

A Non-Medical "Drama"

On top of medical matters, I had to deal with a human resources issue during the last cruise. One of the nurses came to see me. With tears in her eyes, she told me that her tour privileges had been withdrawn, which meant that she was no longer entitled to join onshore tours. Well, I never had to deal with an issue like this but, hey, there was a member of my team requesting help. As the head of department, I had to look after my people. I suppose that aspect of my work on the ship fell under the heading staffing / guardianship. First, I listened to her side of the story, which basically was that she didn't know why the privileges had been taken away from her. The next step was to speak with the tour manager to inquire about the reasons for his decision. He told me that a tour guide had reported that the nurse had displayed disruptive and unruly behaviour during a shore tour. I knew the nurse in question quite well and I found this hard to believe. I asked the tour manager in a friendly tone, but with vigour, to have the allegations investigated. The following morning, I received an e-mail that the tour privileges for that nurse had been restored. It may have helped that I mentioned the issue to my fellow senior officer, the hotel director, who is the boss of the boss of the tour director.

An hour just flew by while I was sitting there on the veranda of the Marriott, pondering about events from the last cruise. My drink was empty; it was time to leave and to re-join the good old "Jube". The time after a cruise was also the time before a cruise and I was keen to discover what would happen during the next one.

Wednesday, 10th of July 2002
Onboard M/S Jubilee, Caribbean Sea

Staff Issues

It was a beautiful evening. The *Jubilee* had left the Grand Cayman Islands just a few hours earlier. The ship ploughed its way through a calm Caribbean Sea. I stood at the aft of the Lido Deck and watched the wake of the ship disappearing in the horizon. I had come up onto the open deck to get a breath of fresh air, to clear my head and to make a decision. Sandra, my current lead nurse, was scheduled to sign off and to leave the ship the next day. Alas, I was not sure how, or even whether, I should say goodbye to her as she had caused me (and others) so much sorrow and anguish.

***Doctor on deck, M/S* Jubilee**

The grievances began with little things soon after she had started her position on the *Jubilee*. One issue was the paperwork which had to accompany crewmembers when they saw a specialist on shore. I just filled out the medical bits on this form. Other information, such as the department they worked for and other administrative stuff, was usually added by the nurses.

Sandra constantly demanded that I should complete the whole form. However, that was impractical considering my workload and the fact that I was the only doctor onboard. There were three nurses who could share the admin side of things. The opening hours of the infirmary was another subject of disagreement. There were prescribed but in reality kept flexible to match demand. During port days not many crewmembers attended the infirmary, and most guests were on shore for excursions. Thus, on those days the opening hours were kept short. During sea days I was busy sorting out the different aches and pains of many patients and therefore kept the infirmary open as long as it was needed. Nobody had ever complained and all the senior officers onboard, including the captain, were happy with these arrangements. Nonetheless, Sandra insisted that the infirmary should stay open during the set hours and made a lot of noise towards the ship's management about this issue.

Her own work, on the other hand, was not up to scratch at times. There were various shortcomings. One day a crewmember was waiting to be reviewed by me after a minor surgical procedure carried out on shore. Sandra didn't check whether this guy was comfortable and didn't bother to offer him any pain relief. On another day I asked her to prepare the procedure room to suture a laceration. Instead of having the patient ready and waiting under a sterile sheet, and the instruments well laid out and ready to be used, I found an unopened surgical pack on the trolley and the patient sitting unprepared on the operation table.

And Sandra was certainly engaged in the blame game. If something was not done or went wrong, it was NEVER her fault. She always claimed that somebody else was responsible. A typical situation was when blood results were missing. She accused her fellow nurses of not having organized the bloods, told me that the laboratory had "screwed up" again or that it was me who hadn't asked for the tests in the first place. In any case, it was absolutely fruitless to get into an argument with her. It would just lead to endless discussions.

Lifeboats, M/S Jubilee

A Sigh of Relief

It was really difficult to work with her – to put it mildly. She had changed the atmosphere in the medical department dramatically. All of us used to be happy little bunnies, but since Sandra had joined our team, a lot of moaning and groaning went on in the infirmary. Everybody watched the other to made sure that they couldn't be accused of any shortcomings or mistakes. In other words, she made our lives miserable. But then she did something which "broke her neck" (so to speak). One of the nurses divulged to her (foolishly) that one crewmember was pursuing her inappropriately. Sandra informed not me, the head of department, nor the captain, but headquarters in Miami. More importantly, she didn't even bother to inform the nurse concerned about her action. Of course, HQ informed the captain immediately about the incident and he called for a meeting which was attended by the troubled nurse, the staff captain, and me. I think the situation was handled sensibly. It was decided to provide the stalking crewmember with counselling and to reassign him to another vessel. Sandra was reprimanded for her actions and was scheduled for a transfer to another ship at the end of the current cruise.

Her departure was a great relief to all of us in the infirmary. Nevertheless, it left me with a little problem – I had to say goodbye to her somehow. That was the reason why I had come up onto the Lido Deck. The fresh sea breeze should enable me to clear my mind to figure out how to do that. And in the end, I decided to show some personal strength. Despite of everything she had done I got her a little present. With it came a card stating that although we sadly had our differences I wished her well, which I truly did.

Afterwards, I felt relieved and it was time to enjoy what was left of that evening. Simple pleasures are always the best. I chose to finish the movie I had started watching the day before. It was called *Meet Joe Black* starring Anthony Hopkins and Brad Pitt. The movie was about death – just the right thing for a doctor off duty.

Thursday, 11th of July 2002
Onboard M/S Jubilee, Cozumel, Mexico

What is a QAT?
The QAT – standing for Quality Assurance Team – was onboard. The term QAT was part of the "new-speech". In the good old days this delegation from HQ in Miami was called Quality Control Committee. But "control" sounded too hard in the times of political correctness so the term was changed, like so many others over the past decade. Black people had turned into African-Americans, but they still experienced racism. Nonetheless, at least they had a new label. Handicapped children became children with special needs, who have the same problems as before. No change in substance, just in language. But beware – everybody who violates the rules of the "new-speak" will be flogged publicly.

Bob Dickinson, CEO of CCL

However, it was the QAT which had arrived onboard the "Jube". Who were the members of this elite club? Well, of course the big man himself, Bob Dickinson, the president and CEO of Carnival Cruise Lines. With him came six vice presidents. Upon their arrival at

10:30 am a general assembly of the ship's crew was called. It took place in one of the larger lounges. There we listened (more or less) attentively to Bob's speech. He called his presentation (very imaginative!) "Vision 2002". He talked about the expansion of the fleet which would create opportunities for new positions and promotion. The events of 9/11 were still a topic. He stressed that Carnival hadn't reduced its workforce after this dramatic incident, although there had been a slump in business afterwards. What he didn't talk about was that the salaries had been frozen since then. This was mentioned by one of the crewmembers during the ensuing Q&A (questions and answers) session. In response Bob pointed out that the financial situation didn't allow for a pay rise at present. According to him Carnival was still in the recovery phase from the decline in passenger numbers since 9/11. But he promised a pay review as soon as the financial situation of the company improves (whenever that would be). A steward from Jamaica asked Bob why Carnival increasingly hired staff from Eastern Europe. The CEO gave a slick answer. With the opening of ex-Soviet countries, the international labour market had become increasingly competitive, so naturally more crewmembers would come from those countries. I had heard another version of his issue. Crewmembers from Eastern Europe were mainly employed as waiters, stewards or bartenders. It was rumoured that they were hired and put into noticeable positions to have less visible staff with dark skin.

Many questions during the assembly revolved around issues such as working hours, pensions, contract lengths and promotions. Bob had a smooth reply regarding each of these subjects. He was a sharp and quick thinker, good with numbers and statistics, but in the end he produced just a lot of PR babble. He talked about everything but told us nothing.

Some crewmembers addressed less political and more practical issues such as: Why was there no soap provided in the washroom for the engine workers? Why couldn't someone have a break from their contract at the same time as their partner who also worked for Carnival? How about a shuttle service from the quay to the city in Los Angeles as there was no public transport? But the prize for daftest question was awarded to an American dancer. He asked whether an electric orange-squeezer could be installed in the dancer's lounge backstage. He got laughs all around.

Ship's plan, M/S **Jubilee**

Small Card, Big Topic

A meeting of the QAT with the department heads was scheduled after the lunch break. Subsequently, I sat with the other 14 heads around a table with Bob and his entourage. The first topic we discussed was quite controversial: the hospitality cards. It all had started with an article in a newspaper that had been written by a travel writer. He wrote that crewmembers on

Carnival cruise ships were not helpful and friendly enough and didn't smile. As a reaction, HQ distributed cue cards to every crewmember (including myself). They served as reminder to smile, to wish the guest a "good morning" (in the morning), to "have a good day" (during the day) and a "good evening" (in the evening). Many crewmembers felt that these cards were an insult to any intelligent creature. Besides, it was probably difficult to smile and to appear cheerful when working 10 or 12 hour shifts every day, all week for up to nine months. Nevertheless, Bob told us that the company would continue to focus on that issue. They would employ so called "shoppers", people who pretend to be guests, but were actually monitoring the friendliness of the staff onboard the cruise ships.

Another hot topic that was raised during the round-table talk was that of port-manning. Since the events of 9/11, a certain number of crewmembers had to remain onboard while docked. Their task was to assist the guests in case of any occurring emergency (a terror attack, for example). Consequently, fewer members of staff had shore leave and the rota was a subject of tension. It remained controversial as to who was best positioned to determine which crewmember should be on duty in which port and for how long. Swapping shifts proved to be difficult. In essence, these duties were seen as an additional burden and (more importantly) as pointless. To remain onboard for an event that may never happen was seen by most crewmembers as a waste of time.

As the head of the medical department, I felt obliged to raise a concern about the crewmembers' health. I had observed that members of staff were increasingly prone to get sick or to have an accident towards the end of their contract. Most crewmembers worked on a ship for six to nine months without any break. And there was definitely a link between their increasing exhaustion and ill health. Bob acknowledged that the lengths of the contracts "was not ideal" and that Carnival was aiming to shorten the average duration. *Yeah, right*, was my thought after his statement at the time. Somehow, I lacked the belief in the promises he made.

Walk and Change
The final act of the visit of the QAT was the so called "walkabout". A team headed by Bob consisted of the VP (Vice President) Cruise Operations, VP Hotel Operations and (as the only woman in that crowd) the Senior VP of Air/Sea Operations. This group was joined by the captain, the hotel director, chief engineer and chief purser. I joined them out of curiosity, and nobody seemed to mind. While we walked around the various decks of the "Jube", decisions about changes concerning the interior of the ship were made.

Safety ring, M/S **Jubilee**

The first stop was at Camp Carnival, the nursery of the ship. It was in need of more space. The solution was to block off some of the public area and to give it to the Camp. The

Smugglers Bar required new chairs and the Atlantic Lounge a new carpet. An additional conference room was requested by the hotel director. After a short discussion it was decided to take the space from the restaurant next door to get a new meeting room. And so it went on. Decisions could be made instantly as all the "big heads" were present during that walkabout. No application or longwinded approval process was necessary. Although the tendency of the decision-making became clear to me. Only minor adjustments were authorised which were expected to take place during the next dry dock session. The *Jubilee* was getting old and was probably not deemed worthy of having big dollars spent on its enhancement.

The chief purser led us to a guest cabin to demonstrate a problem which affected almost all classes of passenger accommodation. The plumbing was a major concern. Toilets clogged frequently, the showers had low water pressure and the bathrooms flooded often due to poor drainage. I didn't find out whether the QAT team had a solution for these problems. It was time for my afternoon surgery, and I had to leave the esteemed gathering to attend to sick or just moaning patients.

Sunday, 14th of July 2002
Onboard M/S Jubilee, Caribbean Sea

There's No Business Like Show Business
It was 10:30 pm on the dot when we got comfortable in the fauteuils of the Atlantic Lounge. With me was my sister Helga, who had come to join me for a few cruises, and my new lead nurse, Lesley. We put our drinks aside and gazed at the stage in front of us. The show was about to start. We had taken some of the "crew seats", the first three rows on the right side of the stage. They were not reserved as such but were usually occupied by crewmembers. The performers knew this and they often made special gestures towards that section of the auditorium. It was a secret "hello" from crewmember to crewmember, so to speak.

With my sister Helga

That night *Broadway* was shown, a performance revolving around the shows played in theatres around this famous spot in New York City. The other act performed frequently on the ship was called *Hollywood*, which was about (surprise!) famous movies. Both themes were just a loose string for a lot of dancing and a bit of singing. The program was very colorful and certainly fun to watch – if seen for the first time. Except, I had seen this show many times over and had grown a bit tired of it. Entertainment onboard the ship after work was very limited. On offer were these dance shows, an art auction, a stand-up comedian and of course plenty of bars. Then again, to attend a passenger bar in uniform was a hazardous affair. Once I was identified as the ship's doctor, conversations inevitably turned into a consultation about health problems. The comedian was quite good, but I found it impossible to laugh at the same joke for the fifth time.

The costumes turned the performers into different people. The women (and a few men) looked very different when I saw them in the infirmary. Dancers were special patients as there were essentially athletes. They had to perform physically and mentally on a high level and that made them prone to have more health problems than the rest of the crew. Problems with muscles, bones or the voice were a common complaint from them. Over the past few weeks, the rate of accidents had increased due to uneven parts of the stage. In the end, the whole stage floor had to be replaced. Sadly, that came too late for one of the girls. She broke an ankle during a rehearsal. I had to transfer her to a hospital onshore for surgery. Unfortunately, it was unclear whether she would be able to ever dance again.

The Dancers and their Doctor

All the dancers were very young and body-conscious, always worried about their weight and fitness. This certainly posed a challenge for me as their doctor. It was incredibly difficult to "ground them", meaning to stop them performing. They always wanted to dance and sing no matter what. Frequently I had to speak with John, the Dance Captain, to make sure that don't to go on stage. That was necessary to protect them from themselves. Aged between 20 and 25 years or so, many of them were just young and foolish. For them, being a dancer on a cruise ship was just a great and endless party. And it was the dance captain's job to keep them under control. In a way it was easy for him to keep an eye on his dance crew. As performers they worked closely with each other anyway. And even outside their rehearsals and performances they hung out with each other, like a close-knit family. Nonetheless, there was envy and rivalry between them. But John did a good job of keeping everything together - and the show afloat. Probably because he genuinely cared about his crew.

That night I thoroughly enjoyed the show, especially seeing that Jody was back on stage. She had a wonderful voice – clear but filled with emotion. Her performance that evening was impeccable as usual. Nobody could have suspected that she had a horrendous experience just two weeks earlier. On an afternoon during her day off she had walked across the car park of a shopping centre. As a vehicle passed her a guy tried to snatch her bag through an open car window. Jody was dragged over the tarmac by the shoulder strap of her bag for more than 10 metres. Luckily, she only sustained minor injuries to her skin and muscles but she was in a lot of pain and remained out of action for more than a week. Another crewmember was not so lucky. He had been mugged by a gang and was beaten up very badly. He actually ended up in hospital and was then sent to his home country to recuperate. Like Jody, he was assaulted in broad daylight on his way back to the ship. There were several similar horror stories going around the ship. Crewmembers were talking about muggings, robberies and assaults they had experienced in several American cities. Fred, the hotel director, had lived in the US all his life. He told me that he never walked the streets of an American city because of the risk of becoming a victim of crime. He preferred using his car or a taxi to get around. I myself felt safe enough to walk in US towns – one simply has to avoid dodgy areas and corners. Whenever I see unsavoury characters, I just cross the street or change my route altogether. And I am happy to report that nothing bad has happened to me.

The problem of violent crime seemed to be far away as we watched the grand finale of the delightful dance show. The dancers took a bow in front of an enthralled audience. The lights came on and we made our way to the Crew Bar. There we might meet some of the dancers again – not as performers but as fellow crewmembers.

Grey versus Black Water

I needed a swimming pool-sized margarita to drown the miserable day I had. At least I was able to escape the ship for the evening. With my sister Helga and a few fellow crewmembers, I went to a restaurant on Cozumel. We were about to have dinner, overlooking a lovely garden. I had ordered my much-needed margarita and reminisced about past events. The day had turned out to be quite different from what I had planned it to be. Instead of showing my sister the beauty spots of Cozumel, I had been stuck on the ship all day.

Bow of the M/S Jubilee

It all had started with an urgent e-mail I had received in the morning. It had come from the captain and informed me that an emergency meeting was scheduled for 9:30 am sharp and that I had to attend. As a result, I had to kiss goodbye to the trip with my sister. Instead of enjoying the Mexican sunshine, I was destined to join the round-up of all department heads in the captain's office. We were joined by a small delegation from Carnival's HQ, who had been flown in from Miami just the day before. All of us were awaiting representatives from the Mexican authorities to join us. Before they arrived, the chief engineer informed us about the issue at hand. A few cruises ago, the *Jubilee* had discharged a quantity of waste water while berthed in Cozumel harbour. According to the ship's engineer it was just "grey water", which comes from dishwashers, sinks and the like. He stressed that no to "black water" was discarded which comes from the toilet system and is therefore heavily contaminated. The discharge of the grey water happened by mistake and was corrected immediately once the error was discovered. Thus, just a small volume was actually released. However, the local Mexican government had made a big deal out of the incident and they had called for this meeting. That was not exactly was the chief engineer had said, but it was certainly what he meant – reading between the lines.

After his explanations, we had a short break to get a coffee and to grab a Danish pastry. Then the Mexican delegation arrived; it consisted of four men and a woman. The men wore colourful uniforms, which looked naval. They represented the port authorities and the woman was working for a marine park. The captain chaired the meeting. He gave a nod to the chief engineer to explain (again) what had happened. Although, this time his presentation was far more detailed and included many graphs and diagrams. In the beginning the Mexicans listened fairly attentively. But after a while they started to asked questions and a heated discussion evolved. Although the content of the debate was quite technical, it was held in English, so I was able follow it to some degree. But then the language spoken switched to Spanish and that was the point where I asked myself: *What the hell I am doing here?* I am unable to speak a word of Spanish and the topic was highly technical anyway.

Genuine Concern versus Shakedown

After almost two hours of a heated discussion, the captain called for lunch in the ship's restaurant. The food was of course superb. It so happened that I was seated next to the lady from the marine park. She seemed to be genuinely concerned about the discharge of contaminated water from the ship. She told me that the marine park was not far away from the harbour and explained to me how fragile marine life is and that water pollution is one of the major threats to it. Mexico certainly had many environmental issues – I could see it each time I travelled around the island of Cozumel. Nonetheless, I was not so sure that a few gallons of grey water would make such a big difference to the overall level of pollution. I had the slight suspicion that this incident was being used to milk a big (and rich) American company.

The coast of Cozumel

As we made our way back to the lounge after the lunch, I asked the hotel director whether he had any idea why he and I had to attend this meeting. He replied that he had no clue. And nor had I. So, I asked him to relay a message to the captain that I should be excused from the afternoon conference. My justification was that I had to see patients in the infirmary. Unfortunately, that happened to be true and I had an incredibly busy afternoon.

After work, I caught up with my sister Helga in the restaurant with the beautiful garden. She had a wonderful day driving around Cozumel with some of my friends from the crew. Apart from my swimming pool-sized margarita, I had a large portion of enchiladas. Chewing my dinner and slurping my drink, I listened to my sister's story. They had hired an old VW beetle. (I had one during my student times.) The car had holes in the floor, the gears got stuck at times and the steering wheel trembled like a mixer. Still, it got them around the island. They had visited Mayan ruins, swum in the sea at a secluded beach and had fresh grilled fish for lunch. With envy I listened to her tale and compared her day with mine. Then again, I thought that was a bit unfair. Helga was on vacation and I was at work.

A different type of Ship

It was the day my sister Helga disembarked. As soon the ship had docked in Tampa, she took a taxi to the airport to catch her flight back home to Germany. The 10 days she had stayed with me on the "Jube" had just whizzed by. It was great to see her, to spend time with her. On the other hand, her presence had made me feel a bit tense as I had two jobs while she was onboard. During the past three cruises I had to look after her, to make sure that she had a good time. But I still had to ensure that I didn't neglect my duties as the ship's doctor. So, to be honest, I did feel a bit of a relief when she left.

SS American Victory, Tampa

Nonetheless, we shared good and interesting times during her visit. One of those moments was a tour around the *SS American Victory*. During my home port days in Tampa, I had always thought that I ought to visit this ship. Yet, I found myself in a situation similar to the one when I lived in Berlin, Germany. I didn't visit any of tourist sites there because I always thought that I could do it "some other time", without actually ever doing it. That often changes when you have a visitor. So, on a stinking hot day, my sister and I made our way from the *Jubilee* to the *SS American Victory*. The Naval Museum ship was berthed not far away from the cruise ship. Built in only 55 days she had come into service in June 1945, just in time for the last few weeks of World War II. As a cargo ship, she transported material and troops to various locations. Her later service included the wars in Korea and Vietnam. In 1985, the ship was decommissioned but kept as a reserve and in 1999 she found her permanent home in the port of Tampa. Helga and I entered the vessel via a comfortable gangway and then we embarked on a tour through the bowls of the ship. Everything appeared to be cramped and uncomfortable. Even the ship's surgeon's cabin offered no comfort. There was no air-conditioning – just a tiny fan was installed to provide some relief from the relentless heat. But, hey! This was a US Navy ship, not built for comfort but to win a war.

First the Blood, then the Food

The three cruises I spent with my sister were a mixture of work and pleasure. One night we planned to have dinner at my favourite restaurant in Cozumel, at the Habana Club. We were just about to leave the ship when I got a call from the local hospital. They informed me that one of the crewmembers had been admitted after a bad traffic accident. He had lost a lot of blood and was in need of a blood transfusion. Unfortunately, the hospital's blood bank didn't have the type he needed, so the treating doctor wondered whether I could send a crewmember from the ship as a blood donor. That was a tall order. First of all, there were no records of the blood type of the crewmembers. (Working for Carnival was not like working for the Army or Navy.) Secondly, I didn't have any means of testing for blood grouping. Nevertheless, I took the details of what type of blood was required and then spoke with the HQ in Miami. The on-call physician assured me that he would make arrangements to fly in a few units of the needed blood. Having taken care of that problem, I was finally able to leave the ship.

That evening, the *Jubilee* had docked at a different quay in Cozumel because the wind direction at the usual pier was too unfavourable to berth there. This turned out to be an advantage as the ship was tied up close to the town centre of San Miguel. So instead of making the usual taxi ride, my sister and I just had a short walk to get to the restaurant. After a great meal, we had coffee and brandy and I smoked a huge Cuban cigar. Our chat was about memories concerning mutual friends. What became of him or her? Where did they end up after graduation? Do they have kids now? With an increased consumption of brandy, the conversation drifted into the field of philosophy. What is a good life? And then the big question: What are we doing on this earth anyway? Of course, we didn't find the answer. It seems that life just goes on while we are trying to find a purpose for it.

Nightfall in Cozumel

After all that soul-searching we had to return to reality. The fact was that there was just an hour and a half left before the ship was due to leave Cozumel. Accordingly, we made our way back towards the pier. It was a warm, gentle night, only interrupted by a short but heavy tropical rain shower. I would have preferred to use the remaining time for another drink in a bar. However, my sister was keen to do what many women love to do – to shop. Subsequently, we negotiated a compromise. She visited the shops while I waited in a nearby tavern for her. We made it back to the ship just before its departure, weighed down with quite a few shopping bags.

Sunday 28ᵗʰ of July 2002
Onboard M/S Jubilee, Caribbean Sea

It was "Just Another One"
Another emergency. I had quite a few of them during the past few weeks. That day, I had a guest with unstable angina (a heart condition). I had discussed the case with the United States Coast Guard (USCG) over the satellite phone. It turned out that the flight surgeon and I were in agreement. The patient was NOT suitable for an evacuation via helicopter. It actually might have worsened the state of his health. On that occasion the risks outweighed the possible benefits.

However, two days earlier, the helicopter had come. A young crewmember was complaining of abdominal pain. The symptoms and signs were convincing enough to make the diagnosis of an acute appendicitis. Subsequently, the usual procedure got into gear. The first thing to do was to inform the captain. Then I had to proceed to the bridge to speak with the USCG. Once the decision for an evacuation was made a lot of action took place. One of the officers on the bridge submitted all the nautical stuff to the Coast Guard such as the ship's position, visibility, wind speed, and all that. The aft of the Lido Deck was cleared and all overhead lights and cables were removed in that section. The nearby swimming pool was drained and covered. The fire crew had to report to the touchdown area with the firemen in full gear, wearing their helmets and masks. They were ready with the fire hose in their hands, prepared to fight any blaze which may occur during the evacuation.

US Coast Guard helicopter

While all this was happening, I was busy in the infirmary to get the sick crewmember ready. A few minutes before the of arrival of the helicopter the patient was carried up to the Lido Deck, accompanied by me, a nurse and security. The guards had to clear the way but they did a dreadful job. There were gawkers everywhere. Some of them blocked our way and had to be pushed aside by the nurse or myself. We barely made it through the crowd. Upon arrival on Lido Deck, we were greeted by another huge crowd. People were standing at the railing of the upper decks and along the demarcation line of the landing site. A few were gaping through the windows of the nearby restaurant. For the guests, the evacuation was a great show, something which interrupted an otherwise boring day at sea. For the staff-members (and the patient) the operation was pure stress rather than entertainment. As for me, the evacuation was just another one. The thrill, the excitement of the medivacs (medical evacuations) had vanished. I actually felt tired at the time, but I had to do my job. And with all the routine I had developed during the past evacuations, I certainly knew what to do. Everything was prepared and the patient was ready for transport.

I got It! (Job Satisfaction)

A huge USCG helicopter approached the ship from behind and then hovered over our heads. The noise was, as usual, incredible. The corpsman, a very young fellow, was winched down to us on a thin wire. I gave him a quick run-down of the patient's condition. The stretcher went up to the helicopter and so did the corpsman thereafter. The helicopter then moved away from the ship towards the horizon. Another successful evacuation had come to an end, but I decided to mention the lousy security situation during the debriefing session with the captain.

It almost seemed that appendicitis is a contagious disease. We had quite a few onboard the "Jube" during the past few weeks. The last case had emerged just three days earlier with a dramatic presentation. I just had started my afternoon surgery and invited the first patient to come into the consultation room. A crewmember, a cabin steward, rose from his seat just to collapse onto the floor again. Fortunately, I was able to catch him, helped by a nearby nurse. We brought him straight to our "crash" (emergency) room. He came around very quickly after I started the resuscitation. Then I took his history, examined him, took bloods and did all the other things a doctor usually does in this kind of situation. It was "doctoring" at its best. This is what my profession is all about: getting things done to help a sick human being. It may sound odd, but I enjoyed every minute of it. It didn't take me long to come to the diagnosis of (yet another) acute appendicitis, although the presentation was more dramatic due to a complication (a peritoneal involvement).

I discussed the situation with the captain. Unfortunately, we were way out of helicopter range, so an air evacuation was out of the question. The only solution was to speed up the ship to arrive at our next port of call, Grand Cayman, earlier. But the ETA (estimated time of arrival) was still many hours away. Hence, I had to keep the patient stable with medication and some TLC (tender loving care). I had to stay in the infirmary most of the night, but at least I had a good excuse to be absent from that evening's Penguin Parade.

The ship finally arrived at the Cayman Islands at around 4 am. It was still dark when the patient was transferred into a tender boat. Fortunately, it was a calm night and there was hardly any swell. It helped the bearers of the stretcher and the nurse to get the patient into the tiny boat without any problems. Then the boat disappeared into the dark with the patient and nurse onboard. For a few moments I gazed at the moonlight which was reflected on the perfectly calm sea as a sliver band. I felt content and happy, having done a good job, but very tired at the same time. I decided to have at least two hours of sleep and a long hot shower before going back to the infirmary for my morning surgery.

Friday, 2nd of August 2002
Miami, Florida, USA

Jumping Ship
For a change I woke up in a bed that didn't sway. The bed was in a hotel room in Miami. It felt pretty strange to have slept onshore after almost six months at sea. Congratulations for my birthday on that day came only from me as I was alone in the room.

Arrival in Tampa

The previous day had begun rather early for me, on the other side of Florida, in Tampa. At 7 am I had to appear on the Lido Deck aft, where four officers from the US Immigration Service were sitting at a long table. In front of them were big boxes filled with passports from all over the world. On the other side of the table, dozens of crewmembers stood in long lines, waiting to be processed. All of us weren't going on shore-leave (for that the ship's ID was sufficient), but scheduled to leave the ship and travel on. That meant we had to enter the US "properly". Although I had a valid passport and the correct visa, it was a nervous wait.

"It is a privilege to enter the United States, not a right," I was told once by an US official. The attitude of the immigration officers was accordingly unsympathetic. With a stern facial expression one of them checked my passport and then stamped it. I was allowed in.

What followed was a quick breakfast and a bit of last-minute packing. Then I had to wait for a Dr. Schulz, who was standing in for me while I stayed ashore. I was destined to attend a medical conference in Miami and had been granted 10 days of shore leave. A call from security told me that Dr. Schulz had arrived and was waiting for me at the gangway. With a sigh of relief, I went down to meet him. I gave him a tour of the essential parts of the ship, showing him his (which was my) cabin, the officer's mess and of course the infirmary. There, in my little office, we both had to sign a lot of paperwork. Finally, it was done: the responsibility for the medial welfare of all the souls onboard was transferred from me to him. I was free at last!

A (nice) slow Afternoon

My goodbyes to the nurses were brief as I would return for a final cruise before singing off for good. With a spring in my step, I walked down the gangway, through the terminal and towards the taxi stand to get a ride to the airport. The flight across Florida was short but tremendously bumpy – more like a ride at a fun fair. It was so bad that the food and drinks service had to be suspended. As a consolation I found a book in the pocket in front of my seat. And guess what? It was in German! What are the odds of a German finding a book in German on an American plane? I don't know, but I took it as a stroke of luck. (Or was it a sign?). Anyway, there was no time to read it then. After just 30 minutes in that flying cocktail shaker, I landed safely in Miami.

The following day was the 2nd of August and my birthday. I celebrated the occasion in the bedroom of a fancy hotel, but by myself. I opened colorful little packages and envelopes which had been sent to me by people who had remembered. It must have been quite difficult for all those well-wishers to track me down. For that reason, I was extremely happy to hear from each and every one of them. The rest of the day passed by like a slow-flowing river. I ate, read the newspaper and watched television. And I certainly enjoyed the fact that I was of not carrying a pager anymore. So, whatever medical emergency was happening on the "Jube"– it was NOT my problem anymore.

After the many months of being on-call, I felt exhausted. I used some of the day for a little snooze. After a good dinner (a BIG hamburger from room service) I had regained a fair bit of energy. So, I was able to go through the documents concerning the meeting of the ICSM (Institute of Cruise Ship Medicine), which was scheduled for the following day. Over four days I would meet colleagues from the other ships of the Carnival fleet. Steve, the medial director of Carnival Cruise Lines, had managed to find doctors to provide cover on all ships for that conference – truly not an easy task.

About 20 doctors and a dozen lead nurses had been invited to attend the conference. All of us had been provided with a program in which a number of of the medical lectures were listed. They were to be held at the Carnival HQ, which was just a few blocks away from the hotel I stayed in. Other events were scheduled to take place at the South Miami Hospital. The visit of a Coast Guard station sounded a bit more exciting. A few social elements were also part of the program, such as a BBQ, a dinner in a fancy restaurant and a pub night. I figured that I might even get a bit of fun out of this shore leave.

An Escape

I had an early start to the day. At 7 am I took a seat in the breakfast room of the hotel. As I slurped my coffee and ate a croissant and fruit from the buffet, I pondered over the past weekend. It was filled with a lot of sleep, occasionally interrupted by sessions of watching television or the reading of the book I found on the plane. *Ansichten eines Clowns* (Opinions of a Clown) was the title of the book. It was written by Nobel prize winner Heinrich Boell. Published in 1963, it tells the story of a comedian who had to deal with the remnants of National Socialism in post war Germany. It was heavy stuff to read, but enlightening. The Third Reich is (unfortunately) part of the history of my fatherland. And as a German I have to deal with this aspect of its past.

Dolphin Mall, Miami

On Saturday night I made an effort to leave the comfort of my hotel room. The hotel shuttle bus took me to a shopping mall. During the ride I had a chat with the driver. He was an immigrant from South America. (I didn't dare to ask whether he was a legal or illegal migrant.) Anyway, he was prepared to accept the hard job of a driver. His hours of duty started at 5 am in the morning and lasted until late into the night. And the reward for all these hours of work was a salary below the minimum wage. As we talked the minibus rolled through the faceless streets of Miami. There were no pedestrians to see, just cars. It made the city look somewhat empty.

After a 20-minute ride, the bus arrived at the Dolphin Mall, a huge shopping center. It was like a town of its own, surrounded by large car parks. Once inside, I was baffled by a maze of alleyways and an endless array of shiny shops. The building was a temple to consumerism. Everything and more was on offer. At its center was a food hall. The grub sold there was what makes Americans (not America) so big: hamburgers, pizza, donuts, ice cream and the like. I already had my dinner that night, so there was no need to stuff my face there. Actually, I was looking for the cinema. I had to pick up a map to find the place. Finally, after a 10-minute walk I stood in front of the ticket booth. I opted to watch *Goldmember* with Mike Myers playing the British agent, Austin Powers. The movie was basically a persiflage of a James Bond film. But it was not "my cup of tea" – meaning I didn't like it. The story was confusing, and the gags were coarse, revolving mainly around bodily functions. Still, for a few hours I had managed to escape the confinement of the hotel room.

Medicals and Parachuting

But the weekend was over and I had to face work again. Well, not work as such, but a doctor's conference. After the early breakfast I merely had to walk two blocks to get to the Carnival headquarters. Once I got my visitor's pass, I went straight to the conference center. There I saw quite a few familiar faces, like Stephen Moran. Stephen was the colleague who showed me the ropes on the *M/S Victory* a few months earlier. His wife, Samantha, who worked as nurse on the *Victory*, was with him. Manuela Jakobi greeted me in our mother tongue, German. It had been a quite a while since she had handed over the *Jubilee* to me.

More than 40 people attended the conference of the ICSM (Institute of Cruise Ship Medicine). The title sounds grand, but it was actually just the gathering of doctors and lead nurses from Carnival cruise ships. I suppose this "Institute" was set up for tax purposes. Still, it was an international gathering as the participants came from different parts of the world including Australia, Germany, South Africa and Great Britain. My colleagues had diverse professional backgrounds: anesthetists, ophthalmologists, surgeons and general practitioners (like me). We all worked on Carnival cruise ships. It so happened that I met my successor, Dr. Rosemary Duby from England. She was quite young and had just recently finished her training in general practice. She must have been quite brave to work as a ship's doctor without much experience. She was destined to find out that working on a ship as the sole doctor can be quite tough. There is no colleague at hand to ask for advice or to "have a quick look at that patient." However, she had decided take the plunge. After the conference I was meant to pass on my duties on the *Jubilee* to her.

Headquarters of CCL, Miami

Steve, the medical director of Carnival, welcomed us all and kicked off the conference. The topics presented that day were not exactly thrilling. The day started with rules and regulations concerning safety management. What followed was a presentation delivered by Danielle from crew medical. She explained how the health of crewmembers was ensured and monitored. Part of it was that every crewmember had to present a medical when boarding a Carnival cruise ship. It stated the results of a physical examination by a doctor and a recent chest x-ray. I saw many of these medicals which were carried out in different parts of the world. They were all in English, but the quality varied greatly, although they followed a stipulated format. My colleagues and I asked Danielle some tough questions, such as: Are the doctors who do them accredited? Is someone at HQ checking them and their quality? I (and many of my colleagues) had the suspicion that some crewmembers simply bought them in their country of origin.

After the morning session all participants of the conference moved to the canteen for lunch. Nothing exciting to eat there – and we had to pay for it (!). We thought we had a boring morning, but we didn't know what was in store for us in the afternoon. We spent four hours with lawyers. They presented various legal topics such as "Legal aspects of Maritime Medicine". The emphasis of their talks was of course to avoid litigation. Actually, my American colleagues were quite relaxed about getting sued. Personally, I would be petrified if I had to appear in court. A US physician described court proceedings to me with the following words: "Being sued is like parachuting. If you have done it once, then you know what's coming the next time."

Participants of the ICSM Conference

A Bit of R&R (Rest & Recreation)

After a hard day at the HQ, the fun part of the conference began: the official dinner. Most participants of the conference had decided to attend. At around 6 pm we were ferried to one of the classiest restaurants in Miami. The dinner was on Carnival, so we were set for a good night. The food was exquisite and so was the wine served. It so happened that I was sitting next to Manuela Jakobi and we engaged in a lively conversation. Of course, we reminisced about the good old *Jubilee*. Manuela had changed from the *Jubilee* to a larger vessel – a two-doctor ship. There are advantages and disadvantages with this kind of position, like with everything in life. The major benefit of having a colleague onboard is that the burden of the on-call duties is shared. That meant that Manuela had a life without the pager and a two-way radio every second day. If she fancied to go ashore, getting stupidly drunk and sleeping the hangover off the next day, she could do so. (Not to say that she did.) On the other hand, she had to get along with her colleague. And that can be a difficult undertaking at times – so she told me. On balance, I didn't envy her. Yes, she had a co-worker for support, but I preferred to be my own boss. It allowed me to run the medical department according to my preferences.

As the evening went on, I seized the opportunity to talk with various colleagues. It felt good to speak with people who understood exactly what one was talking about. We were all (almost literally) in the same boat. So, over wine, whiskey and brandy we exchanged our experiences on the ships and many hilarious anecdotes. Around midnight the nice evening came to an end and a shuttle bus took us back to our hotels. Another conference day was waiting for us in a few hours.

Q&A – Without the Answers

Most participants of the ICSM conference went into its second day sleep-deprived and possibly with a headache. Nonetheless, but we had to pull ourselves together as we were meeting the "big cheese", Bob Dickinson. The CEO of Carnival Cruise Lines joined the conference for a Q&A session. The first question was about colors and stripes. One of the doctors felt that it was important to discuss what insignia a ship's doctor should wear with the uniform. Having dealt with this matter, the discussion moved on to more substantial issues. For instance, the fact that guests have to pay for medical expenses when they get sick onboard. Time and again the situation arose that a sick patient couldn't be evacuated from a vessel because the necessary funds for the treatment onshore were not secured. On one occasion I had an ambulance crew in the infirmary who flat-out refused to take a patient to a public (!) hospital because the transport was not paid for. I had to get cash from the purser to pay the paramedics on the spot in order to get the patient into the ambulance.

The situation was even more dire when an admission to a private hospital was required. In Mexico and on most islands of the Caribbean, hospitals that offer decent treatment are private and they demand huge deposits in order to accept a patient. It was then up to the patient or the relatives to find the money and that often delayed the transfer to a hospital for many hours. To avoid all these problems, Bob was asked whether Carnival could obtain a kind of group insurance which would cover the costs of medical emergencies. The premium for this insurance could be incorporated into the price for a cruise, which probably would be only a few dollars. Bob answered like Radio Erivan: in principle, yes, but in reality, it is not possible. According to him, there was no scope to increase the ticket prices for a cruise even by a small margin. He pointed out that after the events of 9/11, the market for cruises became very tight and that any price increase would not be tolerated by the consumer. So that was that. The remainder of the Q&A session was equally fruitless. We heard a lot of PR babble but no real answers or solutions to the issues raised.

USCG Station, Miami

There was more to It (than I thought)

The afternoon was far more exciting. Following lunch, all conference participants were herded into a coach. After an hour's ride we arrived at the Coast Guard Air Station, where we were greeted for our official visit. A presentation in the conference room gave us an overview of the responsibilities of the USCG. We learnt that the guys there had far more to do than to get sick passengers off a cruise ship. Their duties include chasing smugglers and illegal immigrants as well as being on the lookout for pollution from ships. And, of course, they were involved in the fight against terrorism (which had become a hot topic since the events of 9/11).

From a doctor's point of view, the talk of the flight surgeon was the most enlightening presentation. He provided valuable insight about the complex decision-making process whether to evacuate a patient from a cruise ship – or not. There were far more factors involved than just the patient's medical condition. Many questions have to be answered: Which asset (helicopter) is available? Where is it? Can it be refueled? What is the position of the cruise ship? What is the weight of the patient? Is a nurse escort needed? The weight to transport determines the fuel consumption and therefore the range of the aircraft. And there is also the issue of where to transfer the patient to. It only makes sense to evacuate a sick person if the hospital in range offers a higher level of care than what the ship can provide. But the most important factors are, of course, the weather conditions. On hearing all this, I began to appreciate that I sometimes had to wait quite a while to get a decision from the USCG regarding an evacuation request.

The Worries of the Pilots

During a coffee break, I met some of the helicopter pilots. They told me their worries in relation to an evacuation from a cruise ship. At the top of their list were loose objects lying around on the deck. The helicopter's rotor blades create a huge air turbulence when the copter hovers over the ship. Loose objects may become airborne and hit the engine which would have catastrophic consequences.

Meeting USCG pilots

Another thing I learnt from them, was the reason why they circle around the ship several times before they winch the corpsman down. The helicopter has to approach the vessel at an ideal angle against the air stream to ensure a secure procedure. During my conversations with the pilots, everyone voiced the same specific request: to ensure that flash photography is banned during night evacuations. Since they wear night-vision goggles during the hours of darkness, any flashing blinds them for a few moments, which can create a dangerous situation. I promised them to spread the word that appropriate announcements will be made in future evacuations. How much it will help is another matter. Guests just love to take photos during medical evacuations. To witness a USCG helicopter in action adds to the excitement of their cruise.

Getting inside to get an Insight

After the coffee, we met the stars of the USCG base: the helicopters. It was just a short walk from the office building over to the hangar. Half a dozen airframes occupied the huge hall. The pilots explained to us that they use two types of helicopters for medical evacuations: the Sikorsky HC 60 and HC 65. The latter is a bit bigger and has a greater range (120 versus 250 nm). Onboard a helicopter were usually four crewmembers: the pilot and co-pilot, the winch-man and the rescue swimmer (corpsman).

Sikorsky HC 65, USCG Miami

We were not only shown the different helicopters but allowed to enter them. I opted to climb into a HC 65. The airframes may have looked big from the outside, but the space inside was very cramped. To accommodate a stretcher with a patient was quite tricky. The interior was incredibly bare and there was certainly no space for any fancy medical equipment. On seeing this, I understood why a cardiac monitor had to be placed between the legs of the patient. These helicopters were constructed to be transporters, not air ambulances. Next, I took the seat of the pilot. Again, I was in for a big surprise. Not only the space, but also the view was fairly restricted. It must be quite a challenge to execute difficult maneuvers, such as hovering over a cruise ship to winch down a corpsman.

Mike, corpsman USCG

Good Luck, Mike!

The final part of the visit of the USCG station was a social event. The personnel of the station had arranged for a BBQ. A little garden with a view over the airstrip in the red evening sun provided the perfect venue for it. There was plenty of meat on the grill and an endless supply of beer and soft drinks. As I was munching a couple of spare-ribs I got into a conversation with

Mike, who was one of the rescue swimmers. He put me in the picture regarding the stresses of his job. He had to pass a fitness test every single week since he joined the Coast Guard. And he disclosed that the operations, he was involved in, were not only physically demanding, but often extremely dangerous. Mike had been with the US Navy before he transferred to the USCG. He told me that he was very happy with his current position but noticed that the missions were getting harder for him over the years. His line of work was also not good for family life as he frequently didn't see his wife and his two little daughters for weeks on end. That evening he confessed to me that he was thinking of leaving the Coast Guard to join the State Troopers (a state-wide police force). I wished him good luck and we had a stiff drink (straight bourbon) to that effect.

The remaining days of the conference were not as exciting. Topics covered included how to deal with heart attacks and dive accidents. We learned what the role of the USPH (public health authority) is when a ship has an outbreak of an infectious disease. A biologist gave a lecture about marine envenomation. I didn't know that there are quite a few venomous fish, snakes and other dangerous creatures swimming in the Caribbean Sea. Besides lectures, a few practical exercises also took place. For example, one session involved cutting pig throats to practice how to establish an emergency airway. The life support course had also a lot of practical elements. The four days of ISCM conference were tightly packed with all sorts of maritime and medical topics. The final event was a party in an ale house. However, I didn't stay long that evening, as I had to catch an early flight back to Tampa the next morning.

Thursday, 15th of August 2002
Tampa, Florida, USA

The End is Nigh
Around 9 am on 15 August 2002, I enjoyed a cafe latte at my favorite place in Tampa. It was Joffrey's coffee shop just outside the harbor terminal. My luggage was scattered around the table as I was due to be picked up for a little vacation to get away from it all. My six months as a ship's doctor had come to an end that very day.

Joffrey's, Tampa, Florida

Two cruises earlier I had relieved Dr. Schulz who had stood in for me during the conference. He and his teenage son, who had travelled with him, had enjoyed their time onboard the *Jubilee* thoroughly. As an ER (Emergency Room) physician based in Miami, he had certainly experienced a completely different working environment. Being a ship's doctor for a week undoubtedly provided him with a change of scene. He told me that being the doctor on a cruise ship, seeing many different ports, was a kind of paid holiday for him. Well, for me, being back on the good old "Jube" meant business as usual.

But the end of my contracted time as a ship's physician was in sight. Just two cruises later I greeted my successor, Dr. Rosemary Duby, in Tampa. She had an introduction at the Carnival Headquarters after the conference had ended. Thus, she had stayed another few days in Miami, while I was already back on the *Jubilee*. Dr. Duby and I were scheduled to sail together for a "handover cruise". During that journey I introduced her to the duties of a ship's doctor onboard. Her berth was on the Promenade Deck, a cabin that was high up on the ship with great views and large spaces. But it was also subject to significant movements when the sea got a bit choppy. Seasickness was certainly a risk for the duration of her stay there. However, she was scheduled to lodge there only for a few days. At the end of the handover cruise, she would move into my cabin.

After Dr. Duby had settled into her cabin, I showed her around the vessel. As the ship was at home port it was "passenger free". We were between cruises and the new guests were not due to arrive until late afternoon. On our tour through the bowels of the ship, I introduced her to crewmembers as we encountered them. The long walk ended at the infirmary where she met the nurses. For one cruise there would be a "new doctor" and an "old doctor" onboard. For me that was a good thing. Shared responsibilities also meant half the workload. To avoid confusion for patients and staff, Rosemary and I worked out a rota. In Grand Cayman I was scheduled to remain on the ship, which would give her the chance to see the island. She had to stay onboard once being the sole doctor. The ship can only anchor in Grand Cayman and maritime regulations stipulate that a doctor has to be onboard during that time. In Cozumel it was the other way around. She was on duty the whole day while I did some last-minute shopping there to find presents for my folks back home. In the evening I had a farewell dinner at my favorite place in Cozumel, the Habana Club. Over past six months, I had spent many happy hours at that delightful restaurant, enjoying food and drink and big Cuban cigars.

Bye-Bye "Jube"

Time flew during my final journey onboard the *Jubilee*. I had to introduce Rosemary to all the ship's procedures and protocols. But I also taught her all the little tricks which made the life as a ship's doctor more bearable. We attended all the meetings together, so I could present her as the new doctor. On these occasions I received the usual talk about my good work for the past six months. The hotel director found some affectionate words of appreciation about my services rendered. They sounded genuine and gave me a good, fuzzy feeling. A leaving crewmember was actually nothing special. With over 700 staff members onboard there was a constant coming and going of personnel. Nonetheless, a change of the ship's doctor was definitely noted by the crew.

As it was my final cruise, everything I did was for the last time. So, I had my last Penguin Parade, and my last dinner at the captain's table and, finally, I saw the very last patient in the infirmary. After that I had other things to do such as packing. Over the months I had collected quite a bit of stuff. For entertainment during my (limited) spare time, I had bought a great stereo system and plenty of CDs. I also had gathered quite a few books and videos, and I was in possession of five sets of uniforms. As a ship's senior officer, I was entitled to a seaman's trunk. I duly filled it with all the items I wanted to see again for my next assignment. An endless array of forms and declarations about the trunk's contents had to be completed. And it took an infinite number of e-mails to explain to HQ in Miami that I didn't yet know when and on which ship I would serve next. Eventually, it was decided to keep the trunk in a warehouse in Miami until its destination became clear. In the end I was not so sure whether that dreaded box was worth all the hassle. The staff captain made the prediction that the trunk would go anywhere but to its intended destination and that I would never see it again. I decided to take that risk.

There was a little farewell party the evening before we were due to arrive in our home port of Tampa. It was just an informal gathering in the Crew Bar, attended by the usual suspects. Of course, all the nurses and my successor, Rosemary, came for a drink and a final chat. In addition, quite a few crewmembers from other departments turned up to wish me well. Still, I was surprised by the appearance of one of the cooks. I had not had many dealings with him, except for the fact that he had been a patient of mine. However, he thanked me with warm words for all that I had done for him and then gave me a little present. That encounter made me quite emotional.

Last drinks, Crew Bar, M/S Jubilee

Early the next morning, I had a quick breakfast on the Lido Deck in the guest area. Avoiding the officer's mess was my way of starting to get away from work. Still, that morning it hit me: I was about to leave this floating hotel which had been my home for half a year. It was the place where I had met people from all over the world, where I had encountered professional challenges, and where I also had quite a bit of fun. However, I was also about to leave behind the stressful responsibility to provide medical care for all souls onboard, the 24/7 on call duty, and the boring meetings. Still, I was sure that I would miss the good old "Jube", which took me around the Caribbean Sea on so many journeys. Even so, it was high time to leave as I was in a state of utter exhaustion. The strain of being constantly on call and the many medical emergencies had taken its toll. After the immigration procedure, I took my luggage to go onshore for the last time. As I walked down the gangway, a mixture of feelings overcame me: sadness, because I had to leave people behind whom I had become fond of; joy, because I was looking forward to a nice holiday.

Sitting in Joffrey's coffee shop, I was on the lookout for my sailing buddy Herman. We had sailed together on his 24-foot boat during some of my home port days. He was about to collect me for a seven-day sailing trip to cruise around the Tampa Bay area. Afterwards, I was scheduled to join a cruise ship again, but as a passenger. I had booked a passage to Alaska, to get away from the Caribbean heat – at last.

As I look back at the time of my first contract as a ship's doctor, I am glad that I recorded my observations and thoughts. Having read the lines of this diary again, I wonder what the buzz was about at the time. It probably boils down to the fact that whatever one does the first time is exciting. The first love, the first car (hey, I am a guy!), the first job – these are events which one remembers for life.

I am now into my third contract as a ship's physician. And yes, I still work for Carnival Cruise Lines. By now I know the game. Thrills have been replaced by routine. My current home port is San Juan in Puerto Rico. From there my ship goes from island to island in the Eastern Caribbean. They are all pretty much the same: small, hot and plagued by poverty, but blessed with natural beauty. Maybe I lack gratitude. While I am travelling the world, many people just move from their grey homes to their boring offices. They have to put up with crowded trains and buses and the whims of the weather. Speaking of which...I am sick and tired of the heat! I would give a lot for a cold, rainy day.

And I have another yearning. It would be nice to enter and leave my living quarters without showing my ID and having my bag x-rayed. I often wonder how nice it must be just to walk out the door, get into a car and drive away while listening to my favorite music – possibly just to join a traffic jam around the corner (I wouldn't mind).

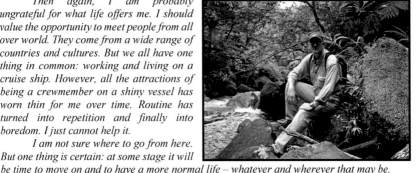

Then again, I am probably ungrateful for what life offers me. I should value the opportunity to meet people from all over world. They come from a wide range of countries and cultures. But we all have one thing in common: working and living on a cruise ship. However, all the attractions of being a crewmember on a shiny vessel has worn thin for me over time. Routine has turned into repetition and finally into boredom. I just cannot help it.

I am not sure where to go from here. But one thing is certain: at some stage it will be time to move on and to have a more normal life – whatever and wherever that may be.

So, my dear reader, I hope you enjoyed the insights into the life of a ship's doctor. In the end it may be just a different way to make a living. Or is it more? It is up to you to judge!

Dr. Werner Schomburg